# Quilting the
# Great Outdoors

LANDAUER BOOKS

# Quilting the Great Outdoors

by Debbie Field
for Granola Girl® Designs

Copyright© 2007 by Landauer Corporation

Projects Copyright© 2003 by Debbie Field

This book was designed, produced, and published by Landauer Books

A division of Landauer Corporation

3100 101st Street, Urbandale, Iowa 50322

www.landauercorp.com  800/557-2144

President/Publisher: Jeramy Lanigan Landauer
Director of Sales & Operations: Kitty Jacobson
Managing Editor: Jeri Simon
Art Director: Laurel Albright
Project Editor: Patty Barrett
Photographer: Craig Anderson and Dennis Kennedy
Photostylists: DeWayne Studer and Laurel Albright

ISBN 13: 978-0-9793711-1-0
ISBN 10: 0-9793711-1-2

This book is printed on acid-free paper.
Printed in China

10 9 8 7 6 5 4 3 2 1

GRANOLA GIRL GREAT OUTDOORS/LODGE LOOK
LIBRARY OF CONGRESS CONTROL NUMBER: 2007926737

# INTRODUCTION

If you're in love with quilts that depict the great outdoor nostalgia, this book is for you.

Featured in the first section you'll find quilts and projects with easy-to-follow instructions and patterns for quilting the great outdoors—an exciting adventure focused on woodland wildlife, mighty oaks and acorns, and nature's splendor—all inspired by my love of the great outdoors.

In the second half of this book you'll welcome nature indoors with lodge-look decorating themes. A unique sampler quilt designed with nine traditional patchwork blocks—each enhanced with its own appliquéd wildlife scene—is just one of many projects you'll be inspired to create.

Choose a favorite appliquéd wildlife scene for a small project or capture the essence of several blocks to create one spectacular wildlife habitat quilt. I hope that you will enjoy quilting the great outdoors as much as I do!

Debbie Field

# Contents

# Contents

## Quilting the Lodge Look 98

## Blocks & Projects

# General Instructions

Assemble the tools and supplies to complete the project. In addition to basic cutting and sewing tools, the following will make cutting and sewing easier: small sharp scissors to cut appliqué shapes, rotary cutter and mat, extra rotary blades, and a transparent ruler with markings.

Replace the sewing machine needle each time you start a project to maintain even stitches and to prevent skipped stitches and broken needles during the project. Clean the machine after every project to remove lint and to keep it running smoothly.

The projects shown are made with unwashed fabrics. If you prewash fabrics, purchase extra yardage to allow for shrinkage. The 100-percent cottons and flannels used in the wilderness quilts and accessories are from Debbie's Granola Girl® collections: Marble Cake Basics, Wilderness Kids, and Out of the Woods fabric lines manufactured by Troy Corporation. Ask for them by name at your local quilt shop

Please read through the project instructions before cutting and sewing. Square the fabric before cutting and square it again after cutting 3 or 4 strips. Align the ruler accurately to diagonally cut squares into triangles. Sew with 1/4" seam allowances throughout, unless stated otherwise in the instructions, and check seam allowance accuracy to prevent compounding even slight errors. Press seams toward the darker fabric when possible. When pressing small joined pieces, press in the direction that creates less bulk.

# Basic Appliqué

Please note that the printed appliqué templates are reversed. Trace and cut the templates as printed, unless the illustrations and photos indicate to reverse the templates. For appliqués that face the opposite direction, trace and reverse the template. Dashed lines indicate design overlap.

Trace the appliqué template to the fusible webbing with a fine tip marker or sharp pencil, allowing space to cut 1/4" beyond the traced lines. Position the fusible web on the wrong side of the appliqué fabric. Follow the webbing manufacturer's instructions to fuse the webbing to the fabric. Allow the fabric to cool and cut along the traced line. Remove the paper backing and follow the pattern placement to position the appliqué pieces on the background fabrics.

Use lightweight tear-away stabilizer to machine appliqué. Place the stabilizer beneath the fabric layers and use a small, zigzag stitch to sew around each shape, smoothly covering the raw fabric edge. If your machine has stitch options, use them to detail appliqués. After the stitching is complete, remove the stabilizer according to the manufacturer's instructions.

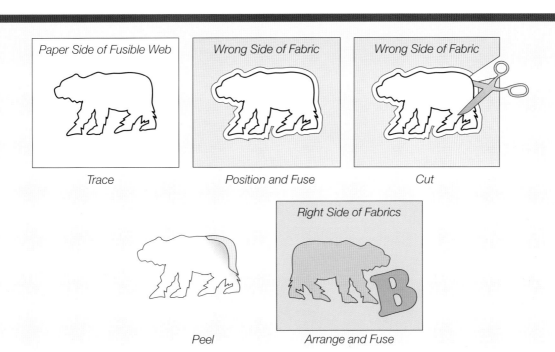

Trace — Paper Side of Fusible Web

Position and Fuse — Wrong Side of Fabric

Cut — Wrong Side of Fabric

Peel

Arrange and Fuse — Right Side of Fabrics

# Basic **Binding**

Join binding strips for a continuous length. Fold the strip in half lengthwise, right sides out, and press. Match the raw edges of the folded strip to the quilt top, along a lower edge and approximately 6" form a corner, allowing approximately 6" free to join to the opposite end of the binding. Avoid placing binding seams on corners. Sew the binding to the quilt top with a 1/4" seam allowance (see Step 1).

At the first corner, stop 1/4" from the corner, backstitch, raise the presser foot and needle, and rotate the quilt 90 degrees. Fold the binding back onto itself to create a miter (see Step 2), then fold it along the adjacent seam (see Step 3), matching raw edges. Continue sewing to the next corner and repeat the mitered corner process. Where the binding ends meet, fold under one binding edge 1/4", encase the opposite binding edge, and stitch it to the quilt top.

Trim the batting and backing fabric even with the quilt top and binding. Fold the binding strip to the back of the quilt and handsew it in place with a blind stitch. Sign and date the quilt, including the recipient's name if it is a gift.

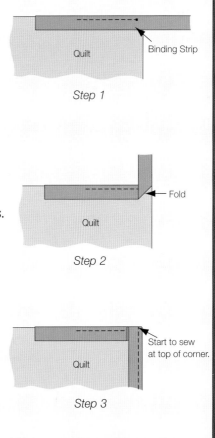

Quilt — Binding Strip

Step 1

Quilt — Fold

Step 2

Quilt — Start to sew at top of corner.

Step 3

# Woodland Wildlife
## Curved Top Quilt

*(Finished size 58" x 88" approximately)*

*Refer to the general instructions on pages 6-7 before starting this project.*

## MATERIALS

| | |
|---|---|
| 1-7/8 yards | Tan Marble for Background Fabric |
| 1-1/4 yards | Black Tone-on-Tone for Sashing and 1st Border Fabric |
| 1-7/8 yards | Dark Gold Print for 2nd Border Fabric |
| 7/8 yard | Dark Gold Print for Binding |
| 6 yards | Backing |
| 64" x 94" piece | Batting |

## APPLIQUÉ FABRICS & CUTTING INSTRUCTIONS

*Patterns for the appliqué pieces are on pages 78-89.*

### Large Acorn Fabrics

| | |
|---|---|
| 1/2 yard | Light Green Marble for Large Acorn Bottoms; Cut 6 |
| 1/4 yard | Tan Marble for Large Acorn Tops; Cut 6 |
| 6" x 9" piece | Brown Marble for Large Acorn Stem Bottoms; Cut 6 |
| 2" x 4" piece | Dark Brown for Large Acorn Stem Tops; Cut 6 |

### Small Acorn Fabrics

| | |
|---|---|
| 5" x 5" piece | Medium Brown for Small Acorn Bottoms; Cut 20 |
| 5" x 5" piece | Dark Brown for Small Acorn Tops; Cut 20 |

### Bear Block Fabrics

| | |
|---|---|
| 4" x 6" piece | Black Marble for Bear Body; Cut 1 |
| 3" x 7" piece | Gold Marble for Ground; Cut 1: Bear Nose; Cut 1 |
| 10" x 16" piece | Medium Green Marble for Blueberry Leaves; Cut 2 and cut 2 Reverse |
| 5" x 5" piece | Blue for Blueberries; Cut 24 |
| 4" x 10" piece | Dark Brown Marble for Small Oak Leaves on Acorn; Cut 3 |

### Buffalo Block Fabrics

| | |
|---|---|
| 4" x 4" piece | Brown Marble for Buffalo Body; Cut 1 |
| 4" x 4" piece | Black Marble for Buffalo Head; Cut 1 |
| 3" x 9" piece | Plum Marble for Mountains; Cut 1 |
| 1" x 1" piece | Cream for Buffalo Horn; Cut 1 |
| 9" x 12" piece | Gold Marble for Aspen Leaves; Cut 12 |
| 5" x 5" piece | Medium Green Marble for Aspen Stems; Cut 4 |
| 4" x 8" piece | Medium Green Marble for Small Oak Leaves on Acorn; Cut 3 |

### Elk Block Fabrics

| | |
|---|---|
| 5" x 5" piece | Medium Brown for Elk Body; Cut 1 |
| 3" x 4" piece | Dark Brown for Elk Head; Cut 1 |
| 3" x 3" piece | Cream for Front Elk Antlers; Cut 1 |
| 3" x 3" piece | Light Brown Marble for Back Elk Antlers; Cut 1 |

| | |
|---|---|
| 2" x 2" piece | Cream for Elk Tail; Cut 1 |
| 2" x 7" piece | Dark Green Marble for Ground; Cut 1 |
| 4" x 8" piece | Dark Green Marble for Small Oak Leaves on Acorn; Cut 3 |
| 10" x 20" piece | Gold Marble for Pin Oak Leaves; Cut 8 |

### Fish Block Fabrics

| | |
|---|---|
| 5" x 5" piece | Medium Green Marble for Fish Body; Cut 1 |
| 2" x 2" piece | Light Green Marble for Fish Mouth; Cut 1 |
| 3" x 3" piece | Coral for Fish Belly; Cut 1 |
| 1" x 1" piece | White for Fish Eye; Cut 1 |
| 3" x 5" piece | Medium Blue Marble for Small Water; Cut 1 |
| 3" x 5" piece | Dark Blue Marble for Small Water; Cut 1 |
| 6" x 7" piece | Light Blue Marble for Large Water; Cut 1 |
| 12" x 14" piece | Dark Green Marble for Pine Sprigs; Cut 2 and cut 2 Reverse |
| 4" x 10" piece | Light Brown Marble for Pine Cones; Cut 8 |
| 4" x 8" piece | Rust Marble for Small Oak Leaves on Acorn; Cut 3 |

### Moose Block Fabrics

| | |
|---|---|
| 5" x 6" piece | Dark Brown Marble for Moose Body; Cut 1 |
| 3" x 4" piece | Medium Brown Marble for Moose Head; Cut 1 |
| 3" x 5" piece | Cream Print for Front Rack; Cut 1 |
| 3" x 4" piece | Light Brown Marble for Back Rack; Cut 1 |

| | |
|---|---|
| 4" x 10" piece | Light Green Marble for Small Oak Leaves on Acorn; Cut 3 |
| 8" x 16" piece | Dark Green Marble for Large Oak Leaves; Cut 8 |
| 2" x 6" piece | Light Blue Marble for Ground; Cut 1 |

### Wolves Block Fabrics

| | |
|---|---|
| 10" x 12" piece | Black Marble for Wolves; Cut 2 |
| 3" x 7" piece | Dark Green Marble for Ground; Cut 1 |
| 8" x 16" piece | Dark Rust Print for Maple Leaves; Cut 8 |
| 3" x 3" piece | Gold for Moon; Cut 1 |
| 4" x 8" piece | Dark Green Marble for Small Oak Leaves on Acorn; Cut 3 |

### Curved Top Border Fabrics

| | |
|---|---|
| 5" x 7" piece | Light Tan Marble for Elk Antlers; Cut 1 back antler and 1 front antler |
| 5" x 6" piece | Dark Brown for Elk Head; Cut 1 |
| 10" x 35" piece | Light and Medium Green Marble for Medium Trees; Cut 3 light and 2 medium |
| 6" x 12" piece | Light Green Marble for Small Trees; Cut 3 |
| 8" x 11" piece | Dark Green Marble for Large Tree; Cut 1 |
| 7 yards | HeatnBond®—Lite |

Sulky® threads to match appliqués

Stabilizer – Lightweight (Tear-away)

NOTE: *Fabrics are based on 42"-wide fabric that has not been washed. Please purchase accordingly.*

# Cutting Instructions

From Tan Marble:
- Cut 3 strips—20" x 42";
  from strips cut
  6—20" x 20" squares.

From Black Tone-on-Tone:
- Cut 10 strips—3-1/2" x 42".

From Dark Gold Print:
- Cut 6 strips—5-1/2" x 42".
- Cut 2 strips—9-1/2" x 42".
- Cut 1 strip—5" x 42".

From Dark Gold Print for Binding:
- Cut 8 strips—3" x 42".

# Assembly

1. Refer to the diagram on page 15 for appliqué placement. Refer to the basic appliqué and general instructions in the front of the book to fuse and position the appliqué pieces to the Tan Marble quilt blocks. Use a small zigzag stitch and matching thread around each shape to appliqué it to the quilt block. Remember to use tear-away stabilizer for stitching appliqués.

2. After the quilt blocks are appliquéd, resquare the blocks and trim so all 6 blocks are the same size.

3. Measure the quilt blocks through the center and cut 3 strips that length from 2 of the 3-1/2" x 42" Black Tone-on-Tone sashing strips.

4. Sew the sashing strips to the appliquéd blocks, as shown, upper right. Press toward the dark. You will have 3 rows of 2 blocks and a sashing strip.

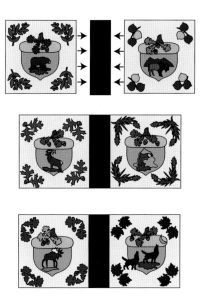

5. Measure the rows through the center for sashing length. Use 4 strips from the 3-1/2" x 42" sashing strips and cut to the length needed. Sew the rows together, as shown. Press toward the dark.

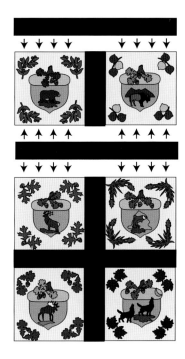

6. Measure the quilt top lengthwise through the center for the measurement of the side border strips. Cut 2 strips to the length needed using the remaining 3-1/2" x 42" Black Tone-on-Tone sashing strips. Sew to each side as shown, *next page upper left*. Press toward the dark.

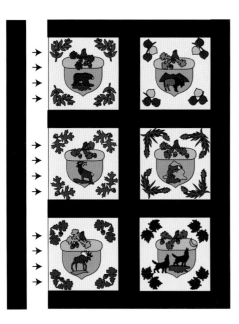

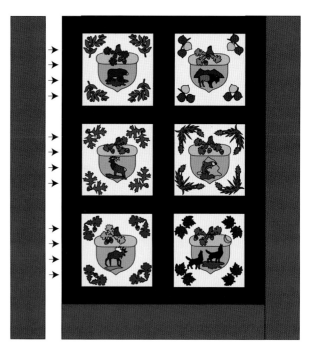

7. Measure the quilt top widthwise through the center for the measurement of the bottom border strip. Diagonally piece two Dark Gold Print 5-1/2" strips and cut the length needed. Sew the strip to the bottom as shown *below*. Press toward the dark.

9. Find the center of the 5" x 42" Dark Gold Print and trace the curved top template on page 86 on strip and stitch on the drawn line. Set aside until Step 11.

10. Measure quilt top through the center widthwise for top border length. Cut the Dark Gold Print 9-1/2" 2nd border strip that length.

11. Find the center of the top 9-1/2" border strip. Place the center of the curved border strip to the center of the 9-1/2" border strip. Sew the 2 pieces together and press toward the 9-1/2" strip CAREFULLY.

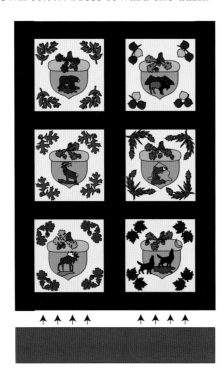

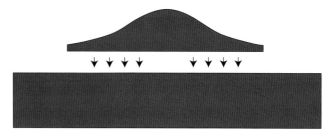

8. Measure the quilt top lengthwise through the center for the measurement of the side border strips. Diagonally piece 2—5-1/2" Dark Gold Print strips for each side and cut the length needed. Sew to each side as shown, *upper right* and press toward the dark.

12. Refer to the diagram on page 15 for appliqué placement. Refer to the basic appliqué and general instructions in the front of the book to fuse and position the appliqué pieces to the quilt border. Use a small zigzag stitch and matching thread around each shape to appliqué it to the quilt border. *Take great care while appliquéing so your border does not get stretched.*

13. Sew the border on quilt top and press toward the dark. Now cut along the drawn and stitched line of top of quilt.

14. Layer the quilt backing fabric, batting, and quilt top. Baste the layers together. Hand or machine quilt as desired. Finish the quilt by sewing on the binding following the steps in the general instructions at the front of the book.

## Curved Top Quilt

# Woodland Wildlife
# Buffalo Check Border

(Finished size 61" x 83" approximately)

*Refer to the general instructions on pages 6-7 before starting this project.*

## MATERIALS

| | |
|---|---|
| 1-7/8 yards | Light Green Print for Background Fabric |
| 1-1/4 yards | Black Tone-on-Tone for Sashing and 1st Border Fabric |
| 2-1/8 yards | Buffalo Check for 2nd Border Fabric |
| 7/8 yard | Black Tone-on-Tone for Binding |
| 5-1/4 yards | Backing |
| 67" x 91" piece | Batting |

## APPLIQUÉ FABRICS & CUTTING INSTRUCTIONS

*Patterns for the appliqué pieces are on pages 78 - 85.*

### Large Acorn Fabrics

| | |
|---|---|
| 1/2 yard | Medium Green Marble for Large Acorn Bottoms; Cut 6 |
| 1/4 yard | Tan Marble for Large Acorn Tops; Cut 6 |
| 6" x 9" piece | Brown Marble for Large Acorn Stem Bottoms; Cut 6 |
| 2" x 4" piece | Dark Brown for Large Acorn Stem Tops; Cut 6 |

### Small Acorn Fabrics

| | |
|---|---|
| 5" x 5" piece | Medium Brown for Small Acorn Bottoms; Cut 20 |
| 5" x 5" piece | Dark Green for Small Acorn Tops; Cut 20 |

### Bear Block Fabrics

| | |
|---|---|
| 4" x 6" piece | Black Marble for Bear; Cut 1 |
| 3" x 7" piece | Gold Marble for Ground; Cut 1: Bear Nose; Cut 1 |
| 10" x 16" piece | Medium Green Marble for Blueberry Leaves; Cut 2 and cut 2 Reverse |
| 5" x 5" piece | Blue for Blueberries; Cut 24 |
| 4" x 10" piece | Dark Brown Marble for Small Oak Leaves on Acorn; Cut 3 |

### Buffalo Block Fabrics

| | |
|---|---|
| 4" x 4" piece | Brown Marble for Buffalo Body; Cut 1 |
| 4" x 4" piece | Black Marble for Buffalo Head; Cut 1 |
| 3" x 9" piece | Plum Marble for Mountains; Cut 1 |
| 1" x 1" piece | Cream for Buffalo Horn; Cut 1 |
| 9" x 12" piece | Gold Marble for Aspen Leaves; Cut 12 |
| 5" x 5" piece | Dark Green Marble for Aspen Stems; Cut 4 |
| 4" x 8" piece | Dark Green Marble for Small Oak Leaves on Acorn; Cut 3 |

### Elk Block Fabrics

| | |
|---|---|
| 5" x 5" piece | Medium Brown for Elk Body; Cut 1 |
| 3" x 4" piece | Dark Brown for Elk Head; Cut 1 |

| | |
|---|---|
| 3" x 3" piece | Cream for Elk Front Antler; Cut 1 |
| 3" x 3" piece | Brown Marble for Elk Back Antler; Cut 1 |
| 2" x 2" piece | Cream for Elk Tail; Cut 1 |
| 2" x 7" piece | Dark Green Marble for Ground; Cut 1 |
| 4" x 8" piece | Dark Green Marble for Small Oak Leaves on Acorn; Cut 3 |
| 10" x 20" piece | Gold Marble for Pin Oak Leaves; Cut 8 |

## Fish Block Fabrics

| | |
|---|---|
| 5" x 5" piece | Dark Green Marble for Fish Body; Cut 1 |
| 2" x 2" piece | Light Green Marble for Fish Mouth; Cut 1 |
| 3" x 3" piece | Coral for Fish Belly; Cut 1 |
| 1" x 1" piece | White for Fish Eye; Cut 1 |
| 3" x 5" piece | Medium Blue Marble for Small Water; Cut 1 |
| 3" x 5" piece | Dark Blue Marble for Small Water; Cut 1 |
| 6" x 7" piece | Light Blue Marble for Large Water; Cut 1 |
| 12" x 14" piece | Dark Green Marble for Pine Sprigs; Cut 2 and cut 2 Reverse |
| 4" x 10" piece | Light Brown Marble for Pine Cones; Cut 8 |
| 4" x 8" piece | Rust Marble for Small Oak Leaves on Acorn; Cut 3 |

## Moose Block Fabrics

| | |
|---|---|
| 5" x 6" piece | Dark Brown Marble for Moose Body; Cut 1 |
| 3" x 4" piece | Medium Brown Marble for Moose Head; Cut 1 |
| 3" x 5" piece | Cream Print for Moose Front Rack; Cut 1 |
| 3" x 4" piece | Light Brown Marble for Moose Back Rack; Cut 1 |
| 3" x 4" piece | Cream Print for Antlers; Cut 1 |
| 4" x 10" piece | Medium Green Marble for Small Oak Leaves on Acorn; Cut 3 |
| 8" x 16" piece | Dark Green Marble for Large Oak Leaves; Cut 8 |
| 2" x 6" piece | Light Blue Marble for Ground; Cut 1 |

## Wolves Block Fabrics

| | |
|---|---|
| 10" x 12" piece | Black Marble for Wolves; Cut 2 |
| 3" x 7" piece | Medium Green Marble for Ground; Cut 1 |
| 8" x 16" piece | Dark Rust Print for Maple Leaves; Cut 8 |
| 3" x 3" piece | Gold for Moon; Cut 1 |
| 4" x 10" piece | Medium Green Marble for Small Oak Leaves on Acorn; Cut 3 |
| 7 yards | HeatnBond®—Lite |

Sulky® threads to match appliqués

Stabilizer – Lightweight (Tear-away)

NOTE: *Fabrics are based on 42"-wide fabric that has not been washed. Please purchase accordingly.*

# CUTTING INSTRUCTIONS

From Light Green Print:
- Cut 3 strips – 20" x 42";
  from strips cut
  6—20" x 20" squares.

From Black Tone-on-Tone for Sashing and 1st Border:
- Cut 10 strips – 3-1/2" x 42".

From Buffalo Check:
- Cut 9 strips – 6-7/8" x 42".

From Black Tone-on-Tone for Binding:
- Cut 8 strips – 3" x 42".

# ASSEMBLY

1. Refer to the diagram on page 21 for appliqué placement. Refer to the basic appliqué and general instructions in the front of the book to fuse and position the appliqué pieces to the Light Green Print quilt blocks. Use a small zigzag stitch and matching thread around each shape to appliqué it to the quilt block. Remember to use tear-away stabilizer for stitching appliqués.

2. After the quilt blocks are appliquéd, resquare the blocks and trim so all 6 blocks are the same size.

3. Measure the quilt blocks through the center and cut 3 strips that length from 2 of the 3-1/2" x 42" Black Tone-on-Tone sashing strips.

4. Sew the sashing strips to the appliquéd blocks, as shown *below*. Press toward the dark. You will have 3 rows of 2 blocks and a sashing strip.

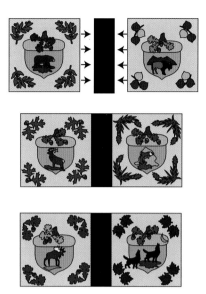

5. Measure the rows through the center for sashing length. Use 4 strips from the 3-1/2" x 42" Black Tone-on-Tone sashing strips and cut to the length needed. Sew the rows together, as shown *below*. Press toward the dark.

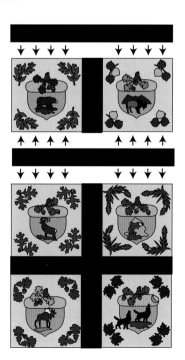

6. Measure the quilt top lengthwise through the center for the measurement of the side border strips. Cut 2 strips to the length needed using the remaining 3-1/2" x 42" Black Tone-on-Tone sashing strips. Sew to each side as shown *below*. Press toward the dark.

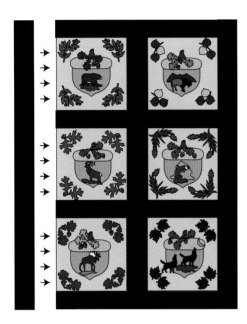

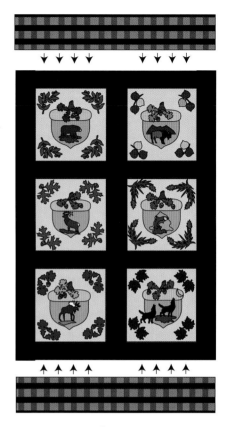

Step 7

7. Measure the quilt top widthwise through the center for the measurement of the bottom border strip. Piece 2—Buffalo Check 6-7/8" strips and cut the length needed. Sew the strip to the bottom and top as shown *upper right*. Press toward the dark.

8. Measure the quilt top lengthwise through the center for the measurement of the side border strips. Piece 2—6-7/8" strips for each side and cut the length needed. Sew to each side as shown *lower right* and press toward the dark.

9. Layer the quilt backing fabric, batting, and quilt top. Baste the layers together. Hand or machine quilt as desired. Finish the quilt by sewing on the binding following the steps in the general instructions at the front of the book.

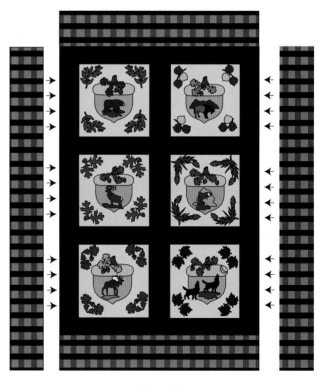

Step 8

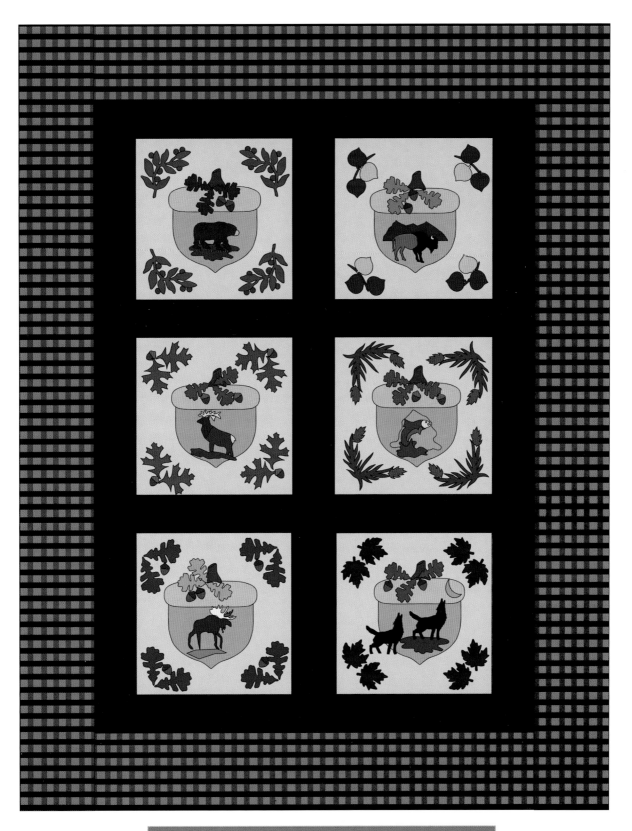

Buffalo Check Border Quilt

# Elk Wallhanging

(Finished size 26" x 26" approximately)

*Refer to the general instructions on pages 6-7 before starting this project.*

## MATERIALS

| | |
|---|---|
| 2/3 yard | Tan Marble for Background |
| 1/2 yard | Dark Brown Marble for Border |
| 3/8 yard | Dark Brown Marble for Binding |
| 1 yard | Backing |
| 31" x 31" | Batting |

## APPLIQUÉ FABRICS & CUTTING INSTRUCTIONS

*Patterns for appliqué pieces are on pages 78 and 81.*

| | |
|---|---|
| 3" x 3" piece | Dark Brown Marble for Elk Head; Cut 1 |
| 5" x 6" piece | Medium Brown Marble for Elk Body; Cut 1 |
| 4" x 4" piece | Tan Marble for Front Antler; Cut 1 / Tail; Cut 1 |
| 18" x 22" piece | Rust for Back Antler; Cut 1 / Pin Oak Leaves; Cut 8 |
| 11" x 11" piece | Dark Green for Small Oak Leaves; Cut 3 / Ground; Cut 1 |
| 4" x 12" piece | Gold Marble for Large Acorn Top; Cut 1 |
| 10" x 12" piece | Medium Green Marble for Large Acorn Bottom; Cut 1 |
| 1 yard scraps | Small Acorn Tops; Cut 2 / Small Acorn Bottoms; Cut 2 / Large Acorn StemTop; Cut 1 / Large Acorn Stem Bottom; Cut 1 |
| 1 yard | HeatnBond®—Lite |

Sulky® threads to match appliqués

Stabilizer – Lightweight (Tear-away)

NOTE: Fabrics are based on 42"-wide fabric that has not been washed. Please purchase accordingly.

## CUTTING INSTRUCTIONS

From Tan Marble:
- Cut 1 square – 20" x 20".

From Dark Brown Marble for Border:
- Cut 3 strips – 3-1/2" x 42"; from the strips cut 2—3-1/2" x 20" rectangles and 2—3-1/2" x 26" rectangles.

From Dark Brown Marble for Binding:
- Cut 3 strips – 2-1/2" x 42".

# ASSEMBLY

1. Sew the 3-1/2" x 20" strips to the sides of the background piece, as shown. Press toward the dark.

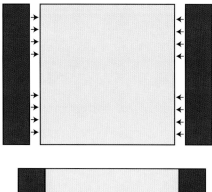

2. Sew the 3-1/2" x 26" strips to the top and bottom, as shown. Press toward the dark.

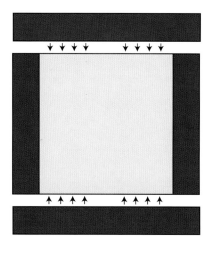

3. Refer to the diagram on page 25 for appliqué placement. Refer to the basic appliqué and general instructions in the front of the book to fuse and position the appliqué pieces to the quilt top. Use a small zigzag stitch and matching thread around each shape to appliqué it to the quilt top.

4. Layer the quilt backing fabric, batting, and quilt top. Baste the layers together. Hand or machine quilt as desired. Finish the quilt by sewing on the binding, following the steps in the general instructions at the front of the book.

Elk Wallhanging

# Woodland Wildlife
## Table Topper

(Finished size 27" circle approximately)

*Refer to the general instructions on pages 6-7 before starting this project.*

## MATERIALS

| | |
|---|---|
| 5/8 yard | Tan Marble for Background |
| 5/8 yard | Black Marble for Tongues |
| 5/8 yard | Backing |

## APPLIQUÉ FABRICS & CUTTING INSTRUCTIONS

*Patterns for appliqué pieces are on pages 90-91.*

| | |
|---|---|
| 18" x 22" | Dark Green Marble for Large Oak Leaves; Cut 8 |
| 18" x 22" | Light Green Marble for Small Oak Leaves; Cut 8 |
| 8" x 8" | Medium Brown Marble for Head; Cut 4 |
| 6" x 6" | Medium Gold Marble for Antler Front; Cut 4 |
| 5" x 5" | Dark Gold Marble for Antler Back; Cut 4 |
| 6" x 6" | Dark Brown Marble for Acorn Top; Cut 11 |
| 10" x 10" | Gold Marble for Acorn Bottom; Cut 11 |
| 7/8 yard | HeatnBond®—Lite |

Sulky® threads to match appliqués

Stabilizer – Lightweight (Tear-away)

NOTE: *Fabrics are based on 42"-wide fabric that has not been washed. Please purchase accordingly.*

## CUTTING INSTRUCTIONS

From Tan Marble –
- Cut 1 square – 20" x 20".

From Black Marble –
- Cut 42 pieces (21 pairs) from Tongue pattern template on page 90.

From Backing –
- Cut 1 square – 20" x 20".

# ASSEMBLY

1.  With right sides together, fold the background square in half, as shown.

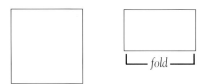

2.  Fold the folded piece in half again, as shown.

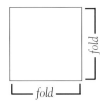

3.  Place a straight pin with a medium–sized head in the corner where the 2 folds are, as shown in Diagram 1. Tie a knot with a piece of string that has been placed under the head of the straight pin. Wrap the other end of the string around a pencil, making sure it is close to the cut edge of the background piece in the upper left corner, as shown in diagram 2. Carefully draw an arc from folded edge to folded edge. Make sure the string is snug, but not enough to move the straight pin. After the guide line is marked with a pencil, carefully trim away the excess fabric with scissors. Repeat step 3 for making the backing.

*Diagram 1*

4.  Refer to the diagram on page 29 for appliqué placement. Refer to the basic appliqué and general instructions in the front of the book to fuse and position the appliqué pieces to the topper. Use a small zigzag stitch and matching thread around each shape to appliqué it to the table topper top.

*Diagram 2*

5.  Appliqué 7 acorns on seven tongues. With right sides together sew 21 tongue fronts to 21 tongue backs, leaving the bottoms open. Clip the curves and turn right side out. Carefully press and topstitch 1/4" from the edge of each tongue. You will have 7 acorn appliquéd tongues and 14 plain tongues.

6.  Place the 21 tongues evenly spaced around the edge of the table topper, as shown. Make sure when placing tongues that you have 2 blank tongues between the appliquéd tongues.

7.  Pin the tongues right side down on the right side of table topper, as shown. Baste 1/8" from raw edge to hold in place.

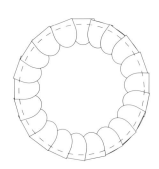

8.  Place the backing and table topper with right sides together, and pin in place. Sew around the edge, using a 1/4" seam allowance. Leave an opening of approximately 8 inches for turning. Clip the curves, turn the table topper right side out, and press carefully. Hand stitch the opening closed. Topstitch 1/4" from edge around the table topper.

Table Topper

# Wool Quilt

(Finished size 49" x 59" approximately)

*Refer to the general instructions on pages 6-7 before starting this project.*

## MATERIALS

NOTE: *Fabrics are based on 60" wide felted wool that has not been washed. Please purchase accordingly.*

| | |
|---|---|
| 2-3/4 yards | Black Wool Felt for Background, Border and Binding Fabrics |
| 3-1/2 yards | Backing |
| 55" x 65" | Lowest Loft Batting |
| 7 yards | HeatnBond®—Lite |
| Size 8 | Perle Cotton (Assorted colors to match fabrics) |

## APPLIQUÉ FABRICS & CUTTING INSTRUCTIONS

*Patterns for appliqué pieces are on pages 78 - 85.*

### Large Acorn Fabrics

| | |
|---|---|
| 1/2 yard | Tan Wool Felt for Large Acorn Bottoms; Cut 6 |
| 1/4 yard | Light Brown Wool Felt for Large Acorn Tops; Cut 6 |
| 6" x 9" piece | Dark Brown Wool Felt for Large Acorn Stem Bottoms; Cut 6 |
| 2" x 4" piece | Light Brown Wool Felt for Large Acorn Stem Tops; Cut 6 |

### Small Acorn Fabrics

| | |
|---|---|
| 5" x 5" piece | Medium Brown or Light Green Wool Felt for Small Acorn Bottoms; Cut 19 |
| 5" x 5" piece | Dark Brown Wool Felt for Small Acorn Tops; Cut 19 |

### Bear Block Fabrics

| | |
|---|---|
| 4" x 6" piece | Black Wool Felt for Bear; Cut 1 |
| 3" x 7" piece | Gray Wool Felt for Ground; Cut 1 |
| 1" x 1" piece | Gold Wool Felt for Bear Nose; Cut 1 |
| 10" x 16" piece | Medium Green Wool Felt for Blueberry Leaves; Cut 2 and cut 2 Reverse |
| 5" x 5" piece | Blue Wool Felt for Blueberries; Cut 24 |
| 4" x 10" piece | Rust/Gold Wool Felt for Small Oak Leaves on Acorn; Cut 3 |

### Buffalo Block Fabrics

| | |
|---|---|
| 4" x 4" piece | Brown Wool Felt for Buffalo Body; Cut 1 |
| 4" x 4" piece | Black Wool Felt for Buffalo Head; Cut 1 |
| 3" x 9" piece | Lavender Wool Felt for Mountains; Cut 1 |
| 1" x 1" piece | Cream Wool Felt for Buffalo Horn; Cut 1 |
| 9" x 12" piece | Gold/Dark Gold Wool Felt for Aspen Leaves; Cut 12 |
| 5" x 5" piece | Light Green Wool Felt for Aspen Stems; Cut 12 |
| 4" x 8" piece | Light Green Wool Felt for Small Oak Leaves on Acorn; Cut 3 |

## Elk Block Fabrics

| | |
|---|---|
| 5" x 5" piece | Brown Wool Felt for Elk Body; Cut 1 |
| 3" x 4" piece | Dark Brown Wool Felt for Elk Head; Cut 1 |
| 3" x 3" piece | Cream Wool Felt for Elk Front Antler; Cut 1 |
| 3" x 3" piece | Cream Wool Felt for Elk Back Antler; Cut 1 |
| 2" x 2" piece | Cream Wool Felt for Elk Tail; Cut 1 |
| 2" x 7" piece | Brownish Green Wool Felt for Ground; Cut 1 |
| 4" x 8" piece | Light Green Wool Felt for Small Oak Leaves on Acorn; Cut 3 |
| 10" x 20" piece | Rust Wool Felt for Pin Oak Leaves; Cut 8 |

## Fish Block Fabrics

| | |
|---|---|
| 5" x 5" piece | Medium Green Wool Felt for Fish Body; Cut 1 |
| 2" x 2" piece | Light Green Wool Felt for Fish Mouth; Cut 1 |
| 3" x 3" piece | Brown Wool Felt for Fish Belly; Cut 1 |
| 1" x 1" piece | White Wool Felt for Fish Eye; Cut 1 |
| 6" x 7" piece | Light Blue Wool Felt for Large Water; Cut 1 |
| 3" x 5" piece | Medium Blue Wool Felt for Small Water; Cut 1 |
| 3" x 5" piece | Light Blue Wool Felt for Small Water; Cut 1 |
| 12" x 14" piece | Green Wool Felt for Pine Sprigs; Cut 2 and cut 2 Reverse |

| | |
|---|---|
| 4" x 10" piece | Rust Wool Felt for Pine Cones; Cut 8 |
| 4" x 8" piece | Rust Wool Felt for Small Oak Leaves on Acorn; Cut |

## Moose Block Fabrics

| | |
|---|---|
| 5" x 6" piece | Brown Wool Felt for Moose Body; Cut 1 |
| 3" x 4" piece | Medium Brown Wool Felt for Moose Head; Cut 1 |
| 3" x 4" piece | Cream Wool Felt for Back Rack; Cut 1 |
| 3" x 4" piece | Tan Wool Felt for Front Rack; Cut 1 |
| 4" x 10" piece | Medium Green Wool Felt for Small Oak Leaves on Acorn; Cut 3 |
| 8" x 16" piece | Dark Green Wool Felt for Large Oak Leaves; Cut 8 |
| 2" x 6" piece | Dark Blue Wool Felt for Ground; Cut 1 |

## Wolves Block Fabrics

| | |
|---|---|
| 10" x 12" piece | Black Wool Felt for Wolves; Cut 2 |
| 3" x 7" piece | Medium Green Wool Felt for Ground; Cut 1 |
| 8" x 16" piece | Dark Rust Wool Felt for Maple Leaves; Cut 8 |
| 3" x 3" piece | Gold Wool Felt for Moon; Cut 1 |
| 4" x 10" piece | Dark Green Wool Felt for Small Oak Leaves on Acorn; Cut 3 |

## Top Border

| | |
|---|---|
| 8" x 10" piece | Medium Brown Wool Felt for Pine Cones; Cut 15 |
| 1/3 yard | Light Green Wool Felt for Pine Sprigs; Cut 4 and cut 4 Reverse |

# CUTTING INSTRUCTIONS

## From Black Wool Felt:
- Cut 6—20" x 20" squares
- Cut 3 strips—5-1/2" x 60".
  Set aside for border.
- Cut 1 strip—9-1/2" x 60"
  for top border.
- Cut 4 strips—1-1/2" x 60".
  Set aside for binding.

## Helpful Hints Using Wool

1. Use an even-feed foot on your machine when sewing.

2. Lengthen the stitch when machine-sewing the blocks together and the borders on the quilt.

3. Press the seams open to reduce the bulk.

4. It may be necessary to use steam when fusing appliqué.

5. Use a utility stitch when hand-quilting the quilt. Utility or running stitches are stitches spaced farther apart.

# ASSEMBLY

1. Refer to the diagram on page 37 for appliqué placement. Refer to the basic appliqué and general instructions in the front of the book to fuse and position the appliqué pieces to the quilt block. Use a hand blanket stitch and matching thread around each appliqué.

2. Sew the blocks together in 3 rows, as shown. Press seams open.

3. Sew the rows as shown. Press seams open to reduce bulk.

4. Measure the quilt top through the center lengthwise for the measurement of the side border strips. Cut 2 strips that length from the 5-1/2" x 60" border strips. Sew to each side and press seams open to reduce bulk.

5. Measure the quilt top through the center widthwise for measurement of the top and bottom border strips. Cut 1 strip that length from the 5-1/2" x 60" border strip and 1 strip from the 9-1/2" x 60" strip. Sew the 5-1/2" strip to the bottom and the 9-1/2" strip to the top. Press seams open to reduce bulk.

6. Refer to appliqué placement on page 37 when fusing the appliqué pieces on the top border. Hand buttonhole stitch around each shape.

7. Layer the quilt backing, batting, and quilt top. Quilt using a utility stitch, and bind with 1-1/2"-wide strips of black wool felt.

Wool Quilt

# Mighty Oaks & Acorns
## Table Runner

(Finished size 15" x 37" approximately)

*Refer to the general instructions on pages 6-7 before starting this project.*

## MATERIALS

| | |
|---|---|
| 3/8 yard | Tan Marble for Background |
| 1/2 yard | Dark Brown Marble for Border and Binding |
| 2/3 yards | Backing |
| 20" x 42" piece | Batting |

## APPLIQUÉ FABRICS & CUTTING INSTRUCTIONS

*Patterns for appliqué pieces on are pages 78, 81, and 84.*

| | |
|---|---|
| 8" x 10" piece | Dark Gold Marble for Pin Oak Leaves; Cut 3 |
| 2" x 5" piece | Dark Brown Marble for Acorn Tops; Cut 6 |
| 2" x 5" piece | Medium Green Marble for Acorn Bottoms; Cut 6 |
| 6" x 10" piece | Medium Green Marble for Small Oak Leaves; Cut 2 |
| 10" x 12" piece | Dark Green Marble for Large Oak Leaves; Cut 4 |
| 6" x 6" piece | Dark Brown Marble for Center Square; Cut 1 (see page 40) |
| 6" x 12" piece | Dark Green Marble for Outer Center Square; Cut 2 (see page 40) |
| 1-1/4 yard | HeatnBond®—Lite |

Sulky® threads to match appliqués

Stabilizer – Lightweight (Tear-away)

NOTE: *Fabrics are based on 42"-wide fabric that has not been washed. Please purchase accordingly.*

## CUTTING INSTRUCTIONS

From Tan Marble:
- Cut 1 rectangle – 12" x 34".

From Dark Brown Marble:
- Cut 3 strips – 2" x 42"; from strips cut 2 — 2" x 34" rectangles, and 2—2" x 15" rectangles.

## ASSEMBLY

1. Sew a 2" x 34" Dark Brown Marble border strip on each side of the 12" x 34" background piece, as shown. Press toward the dark.

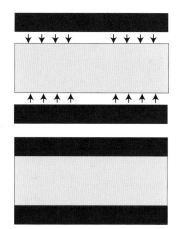

2. Sew the 2" x 15" Dark Brown Marble strips on each end of the quilt top, as shown. Press toward the dark.

3. Refer to the diagram on page 41 for appliqué placement. Refer to the basic appliqué and general instructions in the front of the book to fuse and position the appliqué pieces to the quilt top. Use a small zigzag stitch and matching thread around each shape to appliqué it to the quilt top.

4. Layer the quilt backing fabric, batting, and quilt top. Baste the layers together. Hand or machine quilt as desired. Finish the quilt by sewing on the binding, following the steps in the general instructions at the front of the book.

CENTER SQUARES

Table Runner

# Mighty Oaks & Acorns
## Appliqué Tea Towels

*Refer to the general instructions on pages 6-7 before starting this project.*

## MATERIALS

Purchased Hand Towels

### ELK APPLIQUÉ FABRICS & CUTTING INSTRUCTIONS

*Patterns for appliqué pieces are on pages 90 - 91.*

| | |
|---|---|
| 5" x 6" piece | Dark Green Marble for Small Oak Leaves; Cut 2 |
| 4" x 6" piece | Dark Gold Marble for Acorn Bottoms; Cut 3 |
| 3" x 3" piece | Dark Brown Marble for Acorn Tops; Cut 3 |
| 4" x 5" piece | Dark Brown Marble for Head; Cut 1 |
| 2-1/2" x 4" piece | Light Gold Marble for Front Antler; Cut 1 |
| 2" x 4-1/2" piece | Dark Gold Marble for Back Antler; Cut 1 |
| 1/4 yard | HeatnBond®—Lite |

Sulky® threads to match appliqués

Stabilizer – Lightweight (Tear-away)

### SPRIG APPLIQUÉ FABRICS & CUTTING INSTRUCTIONS

*Patterns for appliqué pieces are on pages 83.*

| | |
|---|---|
| 5" x 6" piece | Dark Gold Marble for Pine Cones; Cut 5 |

| | |
|---|---|
| 6" x 15" piece | Dark Green Marble for Sprigs; Cut 1 and cut 1 Reverse |
| 1/4 yard | Heatn'Bond®—Lite |

Sulky® threads to match appliqués

Stabilizer – Lightweight (Tear-away)

### BUFFALO APPLIQUÉ FABRICS & CUTTING INSTRUCTIONS

*Patterns for appliqué pieces are on pages 80.*

| | |
|---|---|
| 10" x 10" piece | Dark Brown Marble for Body; Cut 3 |
| 10" x 10" piece | Black Marble for Head; Cut 3 |
| 3" x 3" piece | Dark Gold Marble for Horn; Cut 3 |
| 1/3 yard | HeatnBond®—Lite |

Sulky® threads to match appliqués

Stabilizer – Lightweight (Tear-away)

### FISH APPLIQUÉ FABRICS & CUTTING INSTRUCTIONS

*Patterns for appliqué pieces are on pages 82 - 83.*

| | |
|---|---|
| 7" x 8" piece | Light Blue Marble for Large Water; Cut 1 |
| 2" x 5" piece | Medium Blue Marble for Small Water; Cut 1 |

| | |
|---|---|
| 2" x 5" piece | Dark Blue Marble for Small Water; Cut 1 |
| 2" x 2" piece | Dark Gold Marble for Fish Head; Cut 1 |
| 7" x 7" piece | Medium Green Marble for Fish Body; Cut 1 Fly 1; Cut 1 |
| 4" x 7" piece | Pumpkin Marble for Fish Belly; Cut 1 Fly 2; Cut 1 |
| 2" x 2" piece | Black Marble for Hook; Cut 1 |
| 1/4 yard | HeatnBond®—Lite |

Sulky® threads to match appliqués

Stabilizer – Lightweight (Tear-away)

NOTE: *Fabrics are based on 42"-wide fabric that has not been washed. Please purchase accordingly.*

## ASSEMBLY INSTRUCTIONS

1.  Refer to the diagrams on page 45 for appliqué placement. Refer to the basic appliqué and general instructions in the front of the book to fuse and position the appliqué pieces to the towel.

2.  Use a small zigzag stitch and matching thread around each appliqué piece.

# Mighty Oaks & Acorns
# Pine Cone Runner

(Finished size 12" x 42" approximately)

*Refer to the general instructions on pages 6-7 before starting this project.*

## MATERIALS

| | |
|---|---|
| 1/2 yard | Black Felted Wool for Background |
| 1 yard | Flannel for Backing |
| 25" x 47" piece | Low-Loft Batting |
| 1 yard | Lightweight Fusible Web |
| Size 8 | Perle Cotton in assorted colors to match fabrics |

## APPLIQUÉ FABRICS & CUTTING INSTRUCTIONS

*Patterns for appliqué pieces are found on page 92.*

| | |
|---|---|
| 24" x 24" piece | Sage Green Felted Wool for Pine Sprigs; Cut 6 |
| 10" x 10" piece | Rust Felted Wool for Pine Cones; Cut 11 |

NOTE: *Fabrics are based on 60"-wide wool that has been felted. Please purchase accordingly.*

## CUTTING INSTRUCTIONS

From Black Felted Wool:
- Cut 1 rectangle – 12-1/2" x 43".

## ASSEMBLY

1. Refer to the photo on page 46 for appliqué placement. Refer to the basic appliqué and general instructions in the front of the book to fuse and position the appliqué pieces to the runner. Use a hand buttonhole stitch and matching thread around each shape.

2. Layer batting, backing flannel (right side up) and wrong side up of table runner. Sew around the table runner using a longer stitch length, leaving an opening at one end. Trim off excess backing and batting. Clip corners and turn right side out. Press carefully. Whip stitch opening closed. Stitch 1/2" from the edge of the table runner, using a utility stitch.

## Helpful Hints Using Wool

1. Use an even-feed foot on your machine when sewing.

2. Lengthen the stitch when machine sewing.

3. It may be necessary to use steam when fusing appliqué pieces to runner.

4. We used a utility stitch when hand quilting 1/4" around finished harvest table runner. A utility stitch is a longer stitch, on the order of a folk art or primitive stitch.

5. Felted wool is 100% wool that has been washed in hot water/cold rinse, then dried on hottest setting in a dryer. This washing/drying method shrinks and tightens the fibers making the wool useable for rug hooking, quilting, and appliquéing in quilt projects. Always ask if purchased wool is felted. Hand-dyed felted wools give a unique variation of colors to any quilt project.

# Nature's Splendor
## Piano Keys Border Quilt

(Finished size 60" x 81" approximately)

*Refer to the general instructions on pages 6-7 before starting this project.*

## MATERIALS

| | |
|---|---|
| 1-7/8 yards | Tan Marble for Background |
| 2-1/8 yards | Dark Brown Marble for Sashing, 1st Border, 3rd Border, and Binding |
| 1/2 yard | Gold, Medium Brown, Dark Brown, Light Green, and Dark Green Marble for 2nd Border (5 of each color) |
| 5-1/4 yards | Backing |
| Full Size | Batting |

## APPLIQUÉ FABRICS & CUTTING INSTRUCTIONS

*Patterns for appliqué pieces are on pages 78 and 81.*

| | |
|---|---|
| 18" x 22" piece | Medium Brown Marble for Elk Body; Cut 6 |
| 10" x 12" piece | Dark Brown Marble for Elk Head; Cut 6 |
| 9" x 9" piece | Tan Marble for Elk Front Antlers; Cut 6 |
| 8" x 8" piece | Medium Brown Marble for Elk Back Antlers; Cut 6 |
| 8" x 8" piece | Tan Marble for Elk Tail; Cut 6 |
| 1/2 yard | Medium Brown Marble for Pin Oak Leave; Cut 48 |
| 1/4 yard | Dark Green Marble for Small Oak Leaves; Cut 18 |

| | |
|---|---|
| 1/4 yard | Light Gold Marble for Large Acorn Tops; Cut 6 |
| 1/2 yard | Light Green Marble for Large Acorn Bottoms; Cut 6 |
| 6" x 9" piece | Medium Brown Marble for Acorn Stem Bottoms; Cut 6 |
| 2" x 4" piece | Dark Brown Marble for Large Acorn Stem Tops; Cut 6 |
| 5" x 5" piece | Dark Brown Marble for Small Acorn Tops; Cut 12 |
| 5" x 5" piece | Medium Brown Marble for Small Acorn Bottoms; Cut 12 |
| 1/8 yard | Dark Green Marble for Ground; Cut 6 |
| 6 yards | HeatnBond®—Lite |

Sulky® threads to match appliqués
Stabilizer – Lightweight (Tear-away)

NOTE: *Fabrics are based on 42" wide fabric that has not been washed. Please purchase accordingly.*

## CUTTING INSTRUCTIONS

From Tan Marble:
- Cut 3 strips—20" x 42"; from strips cut 6—20" x 20" squares.

From Dark Brown Marble:
- Cut 18 strips – 2-1/2" x 42".
- Cut 8 strips 3" x 42". Set aside for Binding.

From Gold, Medium Brown, Dark Brown, Light Green, and Dark Green Marble:
- Cut 8 strips 1-1/2" x 42" from each fabric.

# ASSEMBLY

1.  Refer to the diagram on page 55 for appliqué placement. Refer to the basic appliqué and general instructions in the front of the book to fuse and position the appliqué pieces to the quilt block. Use a small zigzag stitch and matching thread around each shape to appliqué it to the quilt block.

2.  After the quilt blocks are appliquéd, resquare the blocks and trim so all 6 blocks are the same size.

3.  Measure the quilt blocks through the center and cut 3 strips that length from 2 of the 2-1/2" x 42" sashing strips.

4.  Sew the sashing strips to the appliquéd blocks, as shown. Press toward the dark. You will have 3 rows of 2 blocks and a sashing strip.

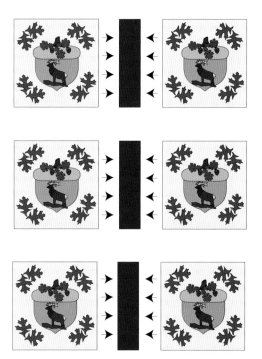

6.  Measure the quilt top lengthwise through the center for the measurement of the side border strips. Diagonally piece 4 Dark Brown Marble 2-1/2" x 42" strips and cut the strips to the correct length. Sew the strips to the sides and press toward the dark, as shown *below*.

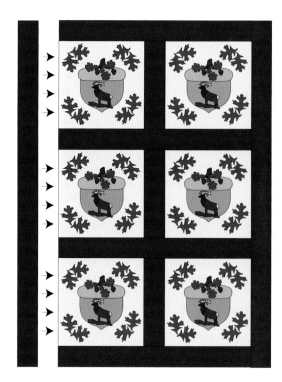

5.  Measure the sashing rows through the center for sashing length. Use 4 strips from the Dark Brown Marble 2-1/2" x 42" sashing strips and cut to the length needed. Sew the rows together, as shown *above right*. Press toward the dark.

7. Arrange 5 of the 2nd border 1-1/2" strips in a pleasing manner. Sew the strips together in opposite directions, as shown, to avoid a curved strip. Press the strips in one direction carefully to avoid stretching. You will need 8 of Unit A.

*Unit A; Make 8*

8. Cut Unit A into seven 5-1/2" x 5-1/2" squares, as shown. You will need 52 of Unit B.

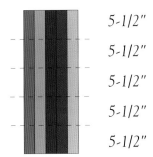

5-1/2"

5-1/2"

5-1/2"        *Unit B; Make 52*

5-1/2"

5-1/2"

Sew 14 of Unit B together for each side border and 12 of Unit B together for top and bottom border. Press carefully to avoid stretching the strip.

NOTE:
*It may be necessary to remove and/or add rectangles to the borders to get the needed length to fit the quilt top. Remember to add or remove the rectangles on the same end of both strips so they are identical.*

9. Measure the quilt top lengthwise through the center for the side border measurement. Cut the length needed from the pieced 2nd border strips. Sew to each side and press toward the dark carefully.

10. Measure the quilt top widthwise through the center for the measurement of the top and bottom border strips. Cut the length needed from the pieced 2nd border strips. Sew to the top and bottom and press towards the dark carefully.

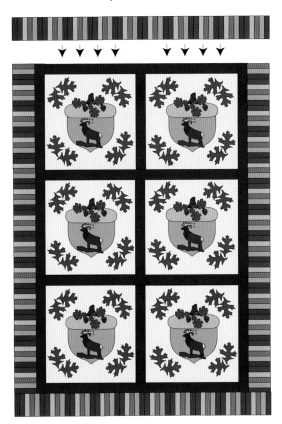

11. Measure the quilt top lengthwise through the center for the measurement of the side border strips. Diagonally piece 4—2-1/2" x 42" Dark Brown Marble Strips and cut the strips to the correct length. Sew the strips and press toward the dark.

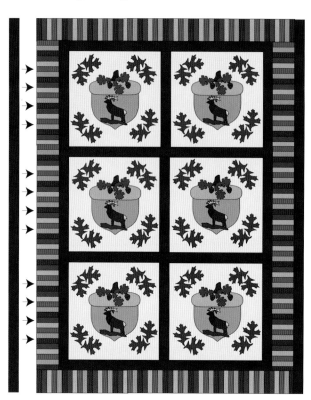

12. Measure the quilt top widthwise through the center for the measurement of the top and bottom border strips. Diagonally piece 4—2-1/2" x 42" Dark Brown Marble strips and cut the strips to the correct length. Sew the strips to the top and bottom and press toward the dark.

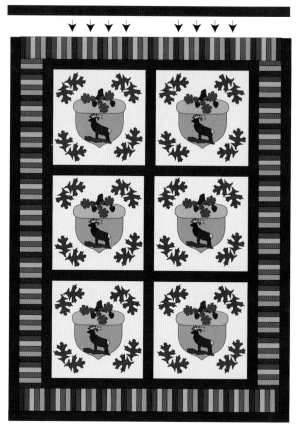

13. Layer the quilt backing fabric, batting, and quilt top. Baste the layers together. Hand or machine quilt as desired. Finish the quilt by sewing on the binding, following the steps in the general instructions at the front of the book.

Piano Keys Border Quilt

55

# Nature's Splendor
## On-Point Snuggler

(Quilt size 50" x 62" approximately)

*Refer to the general instructions on pages 6-7 before starting this project.*

## MATERIALS

| | |
|---|---|
| 1-1/4 yards | Tan Marble for Squares |
| 1-1/4 yards | Blue Marble for Squares |
| 1/2 yard | Dark Brown Marble for 1st Border |
| 1-1/8 yards | Nondirectional Fabric for 2nd Border, *or* |
| 2-3/8 yards | Tree Print for 2nd Border |
| 3/4 yard | Tree Print for Binding |
| 3-1/3 yards | Backing |
| 58" x 70" piece | Batting |

## APPLIQUÉ FABRICS & CUTTING INSTRUCTIONS

*Patterns for appliqué pieces are on page 93.*

| | |
|---|---|
| 1/4 yard | Dark Gold Marble for Pin Oak Leaves; Cut 14 |
| 5" x 5" piece | Tan Marble for Horn; Cut 3 and cut 3 Reverse |
| 18" x 22" piece | Black Marble for Buffalo Head; Cut 3 and cut 3 Reverse |
| 18" x 22" piece | Brown Marble for Buffalo Body; Cut 3 and cut 3 Reverse |
| 1 yard | HeatnBond®—Lite |

Sulky® threads to match appliqués

Stabilizer – Lightweight (Tear-away)

NOTE: *Fabrics are based on 42"-wide fabric that has not been washed. Please purchase accordingly.*

## CUTTING INSTRUCTIONS

From Tan Marble:
- Cut 5 strips 6-7/8" x 42"; from the strips cut 24—6-7/8" x 6-7/8" squares. Diagonally cut squares to make 48 triangles.

From Blue Marble:
- Cut 5 strips – 6-7/8" x 42"; from the strips cut 24—6-7/8" x 6-7/8" squares. Diagonally cut squares to make 48 triangles.

From Dark Brown Marble:
- Cut 5 strips—2-1/2" x 42".

From Nondirectional Fabric:
- Cut 6 strips—5-1/2" x 42".

*or*

From Tree Print for 2nd Border:
- To be cut later in directions.

From Tree Print for Binding:
- Cut 7 strips—3" x 42".

# ASSEMBLY

1.  Sew the Blue Marble and Tan Marble triangles together, as shown. Press toward the dark. You will have a total of 48 half-square triangle units.

2.  Sew 2 half-square triangle units together to make 1 Unit A. Press in the direction of least amount of bulk. Make 24 Unit A.

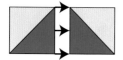 

*Unit A; Make 24*

3.  Sew 3 of Unit A together, as shown to make 1 Unit B. Press in the direction of least amount of bulk. Make 8 Unit B.

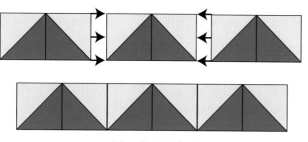

*Unit B; Make 8*

4.  Sew 2 of Unit B together, as shown to make 1 Unit C. Press in the direction of least amount of bulk. Make 4 Unit C.

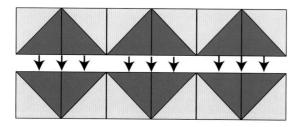

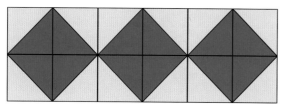

*Unit C; Make 4*

5.  Sew each Unit C together to form 4 rows, as shown. Press in the direction of least amount of bulk.

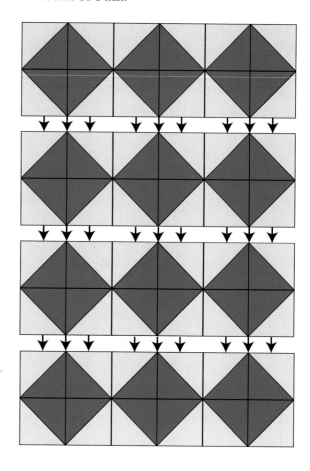

6. Measure the quilt top widthwise through the center for the measurement of the top and bottom border strips. Cut the length needed from the Dark Brown Marble 2-1/2" x 42" strips. Sew the strips to the top and bottom. Press toward the dark.

7. Measure the quilt top lengthwise through the center for the measurement of the side border strips. Diagonally piece and cut the length needed from the Dark Brown Marble 2-1/2" x 42" strips. Sew onto each side of the quilt. Press toward the dark.

8. Repeat Steps 6 and 7 if using nondirectional fabric for 2nd border.

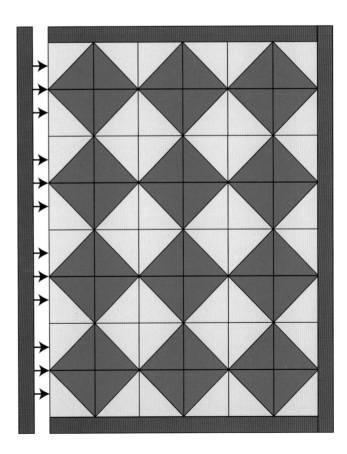

9. Directions for 2nd border using
   Tree Print:
   • Cut 2 strips – 5-1/2" x 42".

Measure the quilt top widthwise through
the center for the measurement of the top-
and bottom-border strips. Cut the 5-1/2"
strips to length needed and sew to the top
and bottom of the quilt.

NOTE: *Remember to sew the strips with design facing up on top and bottom strips.*

Press toward the dark.

10. Measure the quilt top lengthwise
    through the center for the measurement of
    the side-border strips. From fabric cut 2
    strips lengthwise of the tree fabric
    5-1/2" x length of the side border strips.

Sew the strips to each side, making sure
to have design facing up. Press toward
the dark.

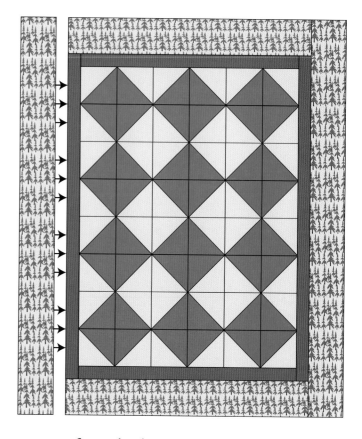

11. Refer to the diagram on page 61 for
    appliqué placement. Refer to the basic
    appliqué and general instructions in the
    front of the book to fuse and position the
    appliqué pieces to the quilt top. Use a small
    zigzag stitch and matching thread around
    each shape to appliqué it to the quilt top.
    Remember to use tear-away stabilizer for
    stitching appliqués.

12. Layer the quilt backing fabric, batting,
    and quilt top. Baste the layers together.
    Hand- or machine-quilt as desired.
    Finish the quilt by sewing on the binding
    following the steps in the general
    instructions in the front of the book.

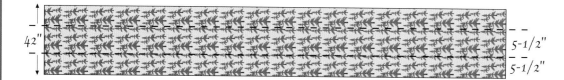

42"                                                  5-1/2"
                                                     5-1/2"

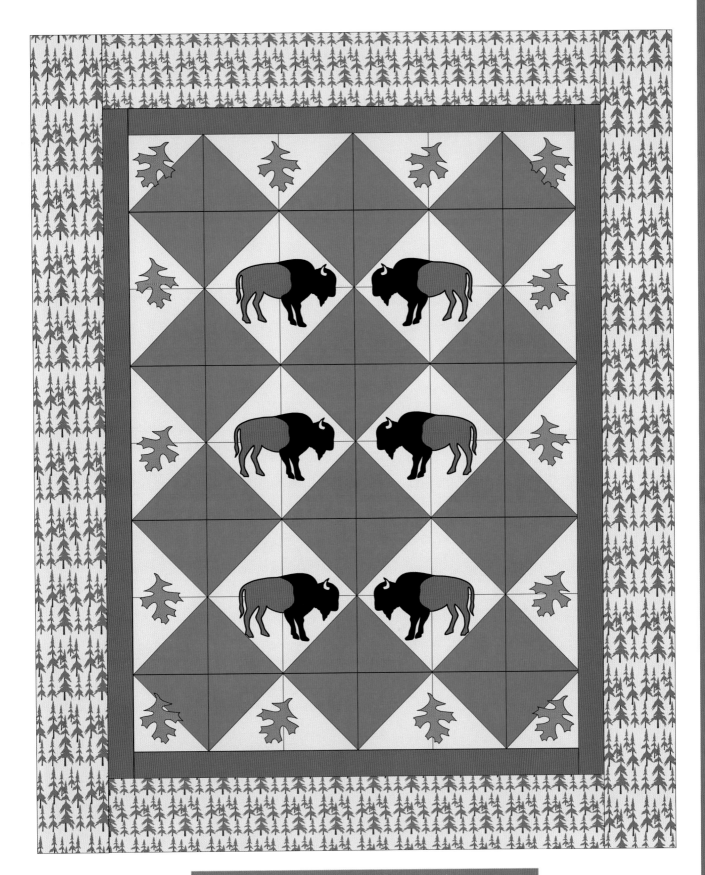

On-Point Snuggler

# Nature's Splendor
## *Wallhanging*

(Wallhanging size 20" x 42" approximately)

*Refer to the general instructions on pages 6-7 before starting this project.*

## MATERIALS

| | |
|---|---|
| 3/8 yard | Tan Marble for Background Fabric |
| 1/2 yard | Plum Marble for Border |
| 3/4 yard | Black Marble for Border and Binding |
| 1-3/8 yards | Backing |
| 25" x 47" piece | Batting |

## APPLIQUÉ FABRICS & CUTTING INSTRUCTIONS

*Patterns for appliqué pieces are on pages 94 - 95.*

| | |
|---|---|
| 1/8 yard | Black Marble for Buffalo Head; Cut 4 |
| 1/8 yard | Dark Brown Marble for Buffalo Body; Cut 4 |
| 4" x 4" piece | Tan Marble for Horns; Cut 4 |
| 1/4 yard | Plum Marble for Large Mountain; Cut 2 Small Mountain; Cut 1 |
| 1/8 yard | Lavender Marble for Small Mountain; Cut 2 |
| 1/6 yard | Dark Green Marble for Tree Line; Cut 4 |
| 1-1/4 yards | HeatnBond®—Lite |

Sulky® threads to match appliqués

Stabilizer – Lightweight (Tear-away)

NOTE: *Fabrics are based on 42"-wide fabric that has not been washed. Please purchase accordingly.*

## CUTTING INSTRUCTIONS

From Tan Marble:
- Cut 1 rectangle—12" x 34".

From Plum Marble:
- Cut 6 strips—1-3/4" x 42".

From Black Marble:
- Cut 3 strips—1-3/4" x 42".
- Cut 1 strip—4-1/4" x 42"; from strip cut 4—4-1/4" x 4-1/4" squares.
- Cut 4 strips—2-1/2" x 42". Set aside for binding.

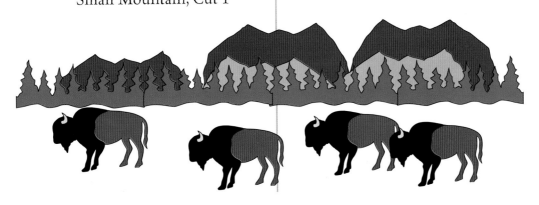

# ASSEMBLY

1. Sew a Plum Marble 1-3/4" x 42" strip on each side of a Black Marble 1-3/4" x 42" strip, as shown to make 1 Unit A. Press toward the dark. Make 3 Unit A.

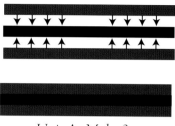

*Unit A; Make 3*

2. Cut two 4-1/4" x 34" rectangles and two 4-1/4" x 12" rectangles, as shown.

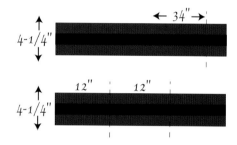

3. Sew a 4-1/4" x 34" Unit A on each side of the 12" x 34" Tan Marble piece, as shown. Press toward the dark.

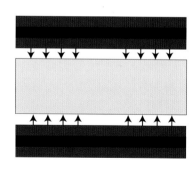

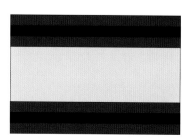

4. Sew a Black Marble 4-1/4" square to each end of the 4-1/4" x 12" rectangles from Step 2, as shown to Make 1 Unit B. Press toward the dark. Make 2 Unit B.

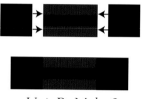

*Unit B; Make 2*

5. Sew the Unit B sections from Step 3 to each end, as shown. Press toward the dark.

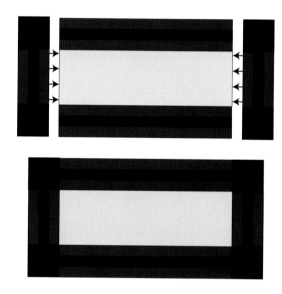

6. Refer to the diagram on page 65 for appliqué placement. Refer to the basic appliqué and general instructions to fuse and position the appliqué pieces to the quilt top. Use a small zigzag stitch and matching thread around each shape to appliqué it to the quilt top.

7. Layer the quilt backing fabric, batting, and quilt top. Baste the layers together.

8. Hand or machine quilt as desired. Finish the quilt by sewing on the binding, following the steps in the general instructions.

Wallhanging

# Nature's Splendor
## Corner Block Wallhanging

*(Finished size 30" x 30" approximately)*

*Refer to the general instructions on pages 6-7 before starting this project.*

## MATERIALS

| | |
|---|---|
| 5/8 yard | Light Blue Marble for Background |
| 1/4 yard | Medium Brown Marble for 1st Border |
| 1/2 yard | Navy Marble for Triangle Square Units |
| 2/3 yard | Light Blue Marble for Triangle Square Units and Outer Squares |
| 3/8 yard | Navy Marble for Binding |
| 1 yard | Backing |
| 35" x 35" piece | Batting |

## APPLIQUÉ FABRICS & CUTTING INSTRUCTIONS

*Patterns for appliqué pieces are on pages 96 - 97.*

| | |
|---|---|
| 18" x 22" piece | Light Brown Marble for Big Horn Sheep; Cut 2 |
| 4" x 4" piece | Tan Marble for Horns; Cut 2 Tail; Cut 2 |
| 3" x 7" piece | Medium Brown Marble for Large Tree Trunk; Cut 2 Small Tree Trunk; Cut 1 |
| 18" x 22" piece | Navy Marble for Mountains; Cut 2 |
| 18" x 22" piece | Light Green Marble for Trees; Cut 4 |

| | |
|---|---|
| 1 yard | HeatnBond®—Lite |

Sulky® threads to match appliqués

Stabilizer – Lightweight (Tear-away)

NOTE: *Fabrics are based on 42"-wide fabric that has not been washed. Please purchase accordingly.*

## CUTTING INSTRUCTIONS

From Light Blue Marble for Background:
- Cut 1 square 18-1/2" x 18-1/2".

From Medium Brown Marble:
- Cut 2 strips 1-1/2" x 42"; from the strips cut 2—1-1/2" x 18-1/2" rectangles and 2—1-1/2" x 20-1/2" rectangles.

From Navy Marble for Triangle Square Units:
- Cut 2 strips 5-7/8" x 42"; from the strips cut 8—5-7/8" x 5-7/8" squares. Diagonally cut squares to make 16 triangles.

From Light Blue Marble for Triangle Square Units and Outer Squares:
- Cut 2 strips 5-7/8" x 42"; from the strips cut 8—5-7/8" x 5-7/8" squares. Diagonally cut once for 16 triangles.
- Cut 1 strip 5-1/2" x 42"; from the strips cut 4—5-1/2" x 5-1/2" squares.

From Navy Marble for Binding:
- Cut 4 strips 2-1/2" x 42".

# ASSEMBLY

1.  Sew the 1-1/2" x 18-1/2" Medium Brown Marble 1st border strips to the top and bottom of the background piece, as shown. Press toward the dark.

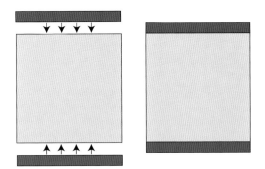

2.  Sew the 1-1/2" x 20-1/2" Medium Brown Marble 1st border strips to each side of the quilt top, as shown. Press toward the dark.

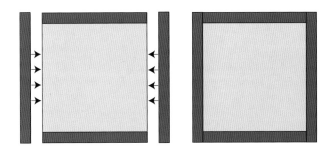

3.  Sew the Navy Marble and Light Blue Marble triangles together, as shown. Press toward the dark.

*Make 16*

4.  Sew 4 half-square triangle units together, as shown to make 1 Unit A. Press in the direction of least amount of bulk. Make 4 Unit A.

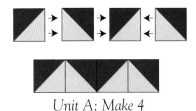

*Unit A; Make 4*

5.  Sew 2 Unit A Strips to the sides of the quilt unit, as shown.

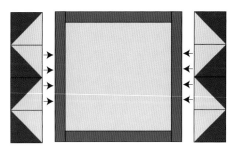

6.  Sew the Light Blue Marble 5-1/2" squares to each end of the remaining 2 Unit A units, as shown to make 1 Unit B. Press toward the square to reduce bulk. Make 2 Unit B.

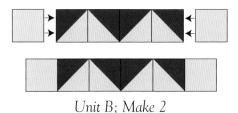

*Unit B; Make 2*

7.  Sew Unit B to the top and bottom of the quilt, as shown. Press toward the dark or in the direction of least amount of bulk.

8.  Refer to the diagram on page 69 for appliqué placement. Refer to the basic appliqué and general instructions in the front of the book to fuse and position the appliqué pieces to the quilt top. Use a small zigzag stitch and matching thread around each shape to appliqué it to the quilt top.

9. Layer the quilt backing fabric, batting, and quilt top. Baste the layers together. Hand or machine quilt as desired. Finish the quilt by sewing on the binding, following the steps in the general instructions at the front of the book.

Corner Block Wallhanging

# Nature's Splendor
## Legends Quilt

(Finished size 80" x 96" approximately)

*Refer to the general instructions on pages 6-7 before starting this project.*

## MATERIALS

| | |
|---|---|
| 3-1/4 yards | Medium Brown Print for 6" squares and Set-in Triangles |
| 2-1/8 yards | Tan Print for Pieced Blocks |
| 2-1/8 yards | Dark Brown Floral for Pieced Blocks |
| 3/4 yard | Dark Brown Print for 1st Border |
| 1-3/8 yards | Dark Brown Floral for 2nd Border |
| 1 yard | Dark Brown Print for Binding |
| 6 yards | Backing |
| Queen Size | Batting |

NOTE: *Fabrics are based on 42"-wide fabric that has not been washed. Please purchase accordingly.*

## CUTTING INSTRUCTIONS

From Medium Brown Print:
- Cut 12 strips—6" x 42"; from the strips cut 80—6" squares.
- Cut 3 strips—9" x 42"; from the strips cut 9—9" squares. Diagonally cut each twice for 36 triangles.
- Cut 1 strip—4-3/4" x 42"; from the strips cut 2—4-3/4" x 4-3/4" squares. Diagonally cut each once for 4 triangles.

From Tan Print:
- Cut 18 strips—3-5/8" x 42"; from the strips cut 198—3-5/8" x 3-5/8" squares. Diagonally cut each once for 396 triangles.

From Dark Brown Floral Print for Pieced Blocks:
- Cut 18 strips—3-5/8" x 42"; from the strips cut 198—3-5/8" x 3-5/8" squares. Diagonally cut each once for 396 triangles.

From Dark Brown Print for 1st Border:
- Cut 8 strips—2-1/2" x 42".

From Dark Brown Floral for 2nd Border:
- Cut 8 strips—2-1/2" x 42".

From Dark Brown Print for Binding:
- Cut 10 strips—3" x 42".

# ASSEMBLY

1. Sew the tan print and dark brown floral print triangles right sides together, as shown. Press toward the dark. You will need a total of 396 triangle-square units.

2. Sew two triangle-square units together, as shown to make 1 Unit A. Press in the direction of least amount of bulk. Make 198 Unit A.

*Unit A; Make 198*

3. Sew 2 of Unit A together, as shown to make 1 Unit B. Watch so that the units are sewn in the correct position. Press in the direction of least amount of bulk. Make 99 Unit B.

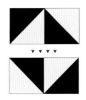 

*Unit B; Make 99*

4. Sew the blocks together, diagonally, as shown in diagram. Press in the direction of least amount of bulk. After the rows have been stitched together, sew the 4 corner triangles on. It may be necessary to trim off the excess triangles to square up the quilt top. When trimming the quilt top, make sure that you leave 1/4" seam allowance past the corners of the block, as shown.

5. Measure the quilt top through the center widthwise for top and bottom border length. Diagonally piece and cut the Dark Brown Print 2-1/2" x 42" 1st border strips to that measurement. Sew to the top and bottom. Press toward the border. Measure the quilt top through the center lengthwise for side border length. Cut two strips that measurement and sew to the sides. Press toward the border.

6. Repeat Step 5 for second border.

7. Layer quilt top, batting, and backing. Baste and quilt as desired.

8. Diagonally piece the 3" binding strips together. Fold the strips in half, wrong sides together, and press. Stitch to the right side of quilt with raw edges matching. Fold over to the back and blind stitch, catching backing of quilt without piercing through to the front of the quilt.

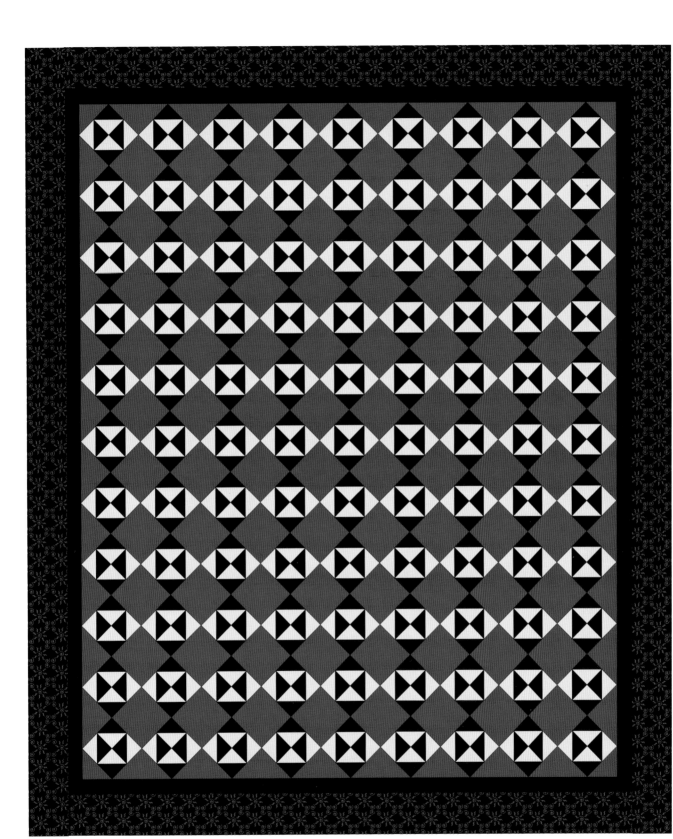

Legends Quilt

# Nature's Splendor
## Legends Pillow

(Finished size 12" x 18" approximately)

*Refer to the general instructions on pages 6-7 before starting this project.*

## MATERIALS

*(Yardage listed is enough for 2 pillows.)*

| | |
|---|---|
| 3/8 yard | Tan Print for Pieced Blocks and Center |
| 1-1/2 yards | Medium Brown Print for Sashing and Back |
| 1-1/8 yards | Dark Brown Floral for Pieced Blocks and Ruffle |

## APPLIQUÉ FABRICS & CUTTING INSTRUCTIONS

*Patterns for appliqué are on pages 78 and 84.*

| | |
|---|---|
| 2" x 5" piece | Medium Brown Marble for Small Acorn Bottoms; Cut 3 |
| 2" x 5" piece | Dark Brown Marble for Small Acorn Tops; Cut 3 |
| 18" x 22" piece | Dark Green Marble for Large Oak Leaves; Cut 6 |
| 6" x 10" piece | Medium Green Marble for Small Oak Leaves; Cut 4 |
| 1-1/4 yards | HeatnBond®—Lite |

Sulky® threads to match appliqués

Stabilizer – Lightweight (Tear-away)

NOTE: *Fabrics are based on 42"-wide fabric that has not been washed. Please purchase accordingly.*

## CUTTING INSTRUCTIONS
### FOR TWO PILLOWS

From Tan Print:
- Cut 1 strip – 2-3/8" x 42"; from the strip cut 16—2-3/8" x 2-3/8" squares. Diagonally cut once for 32 triangles.
- Cut 1 strip – 6-1/2" x 42"; from the strip cut 2—6-1/2" x 12-1/2" rectangles.

From Medium Brown Print:
- Cut 2 strips—3-1/2" x 42"; from the strips cut 4—3-1/2" x 6-1/2" rectangles and cut 4—3-1/2" x 12-1/2" rectangles.
- Cut 2 strips—12-1/2" x 42"; from the strips cut 4—12-1/2" x 12-1/2" squares.

From Dark Brown Floral:
- Cut 1 strip—2-3/8" x 42"; from the strip cut 16—2-3/8" x 2-3/8" squares. Diagonally cut once for 32 triangles.
- Cut 5 strips—6-1/2" x 42"; from the strips cut 2—6-1/2" x 21" rectangles. Reserve 4 strips for ruffles.

# ASSEMBLY

1. Sew the Tan Print and Dark Brown Floral triangles together, as shown to make 1 Unit A. Press toward the dark. Make 32 Unit A.

 *Unit A; Make 32*

2. Sew together 2 Unit A, as shown to make 1 Unit B. Press in the direction of least amount of bulk. Make 16 Unit B.

 *Unit B; Make 16*

3. Sew together 2 Unit B, as shown to make Unit C. Press in the direction of least amount of bulk. Make 8 Unit C.

  *Unit C; Make 8*

4. Sew the 3-1/2" x 12-1/2" Medium Brown Print sashing strips on the top and bottom of the center piece. Press toward the dark.

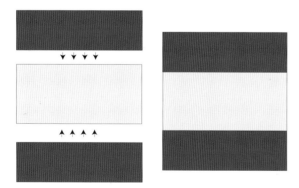

5. Sew the Unit C blocks on each end of the 3-1/2" x 6-1/2" Medium Brown Print sashing strips to make 2 Unit D. Press toward the dark.

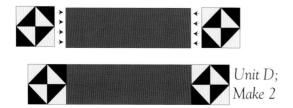 *Unit D; Make 2*

6. Sew one Unit D on each side of the pillow center. Press toward the dark.

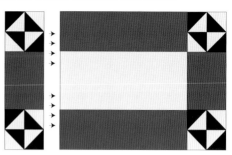

7. Refer to the diagram on page 77 for appliqué placement. Refer to the basic appliqué and general instructions in the front of the book to fuse and position the appliqué pieces to the pillow top. Use a small zigzag stitch and matching thread around each shape to appliqué it to the pillow top.

8. Sew 2—6-1/2" x 42" Dark Brown Floral strips and 1—6-1/2" x 21" strip together to make a continuous ruffle strip. Fold the strip in half lengthwise, wrong sides together, and press.

9. Divide the ruffle strip into four equal sections and mark with safety pins. Sew two rows of basting stitches with the machine having the first basting row 1/8" from the raw edge and the second basting row 3/8" from the raw edge, as shown.

3-1/2"    1/8"   3/8"

*Fold*

10. Divide the pillow top into four equal sections and mark with safety pins. With right sides together, pin the ruffle to the pillow top, lining up the safety pins. Carefully pull the gathering threads until the ruffle fits the pillow top. Round the corners slightly. Sew the ruffle to the pillow top, stitching between the basting rows, as shown.

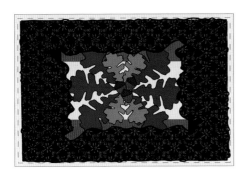

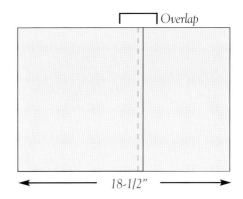

*Overlap*

18-1/2"

11. Sew 1/4" double hem on one edge of the 12-1/2" squares. Press.

12. Overlap two of the 12-1/2" Medium Brown Print squares so the pillow back measures 18-1/2", as shown. Pin together and baste 1/8" from raw edge to hold in place.

13. Pin the pillow top and back together, right sides together and sew. Be careful when sewing front and back together.

14. Turn the pillow right side out, insert a pillow form.

## Legends Pillow

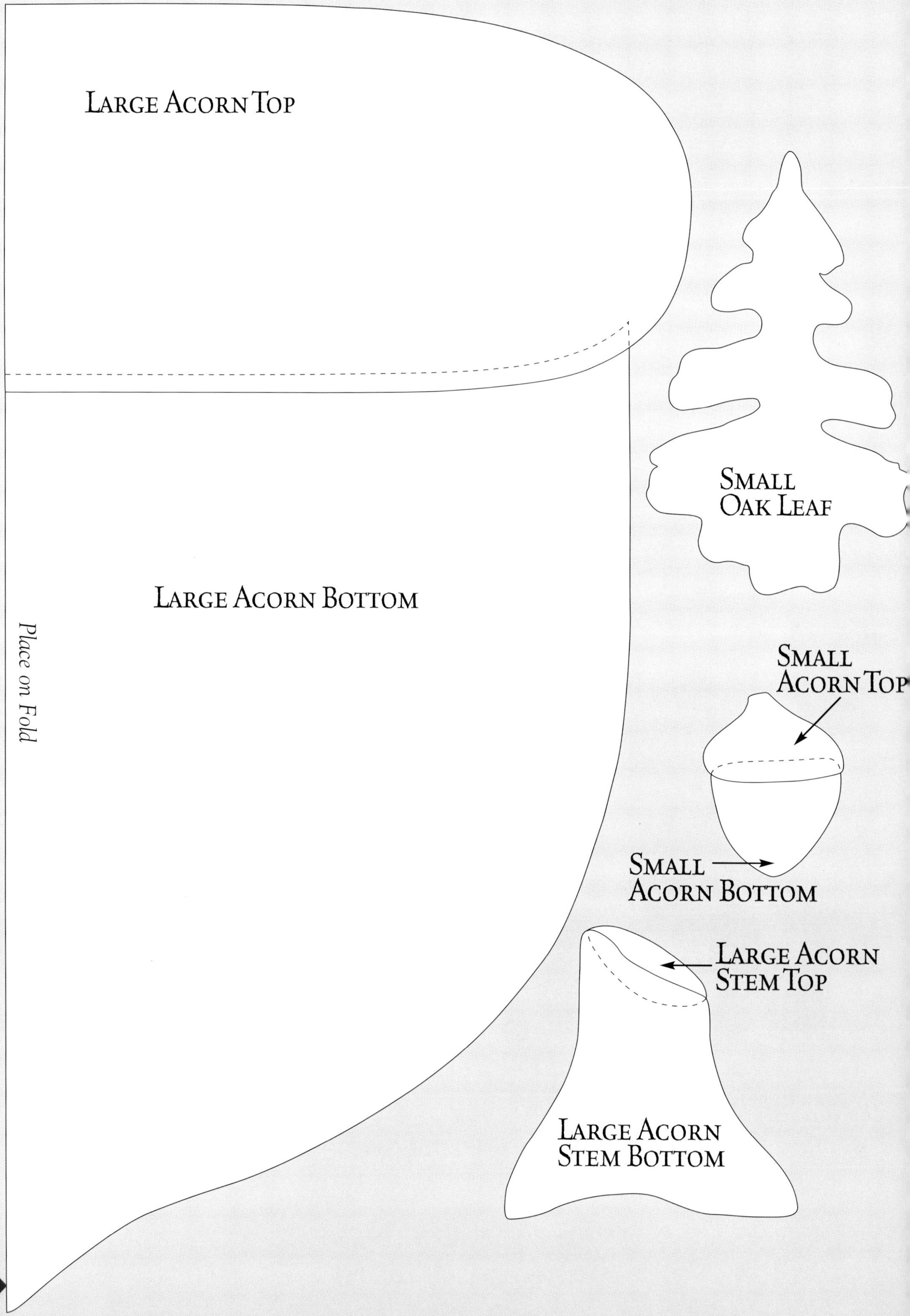

LARGE ACORN TOP

SMALL
OAK LEAF

*Place on Fold*

LARGE ACORN BOTTOM

SMALL
ACORN TOP

SMALL
ACORN BOTTOM

LARGE ACORN
STEM TOP

LARGE ACORN
STEM BOTTOM

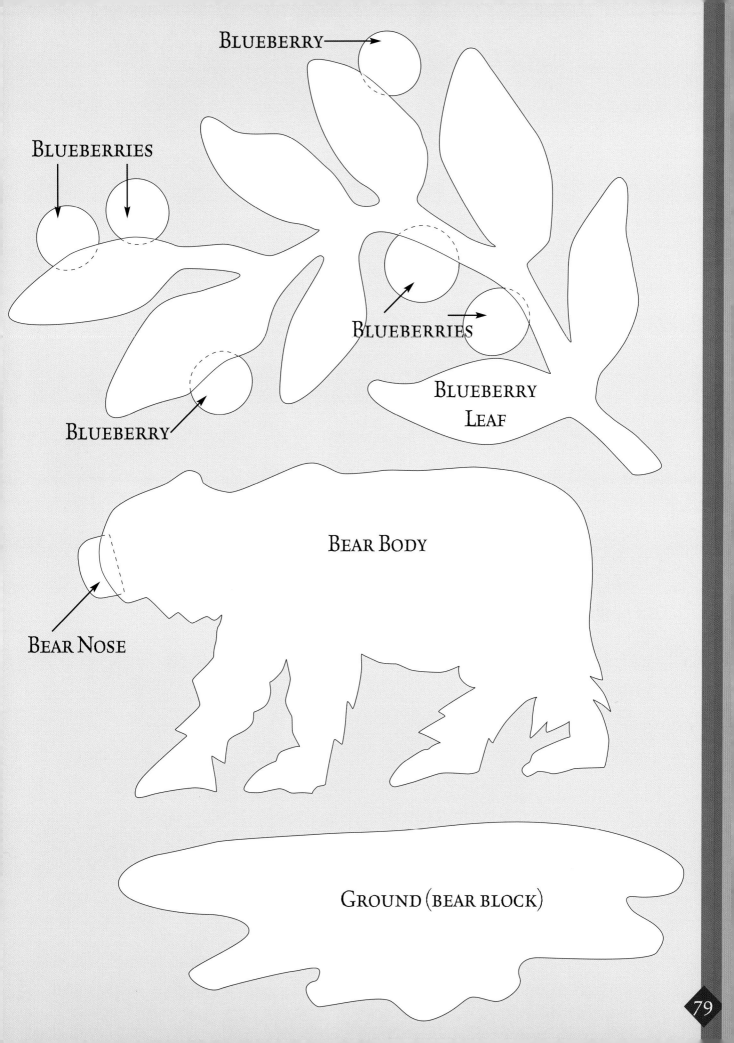

BLUEBERRY

BLUEBERRIES

BLUEBERRIES

BLUEBERRY

BLUEBERRY LEAF

BEAR BODY

BEAR NOSE

GROUND (BEAR BLOCK)

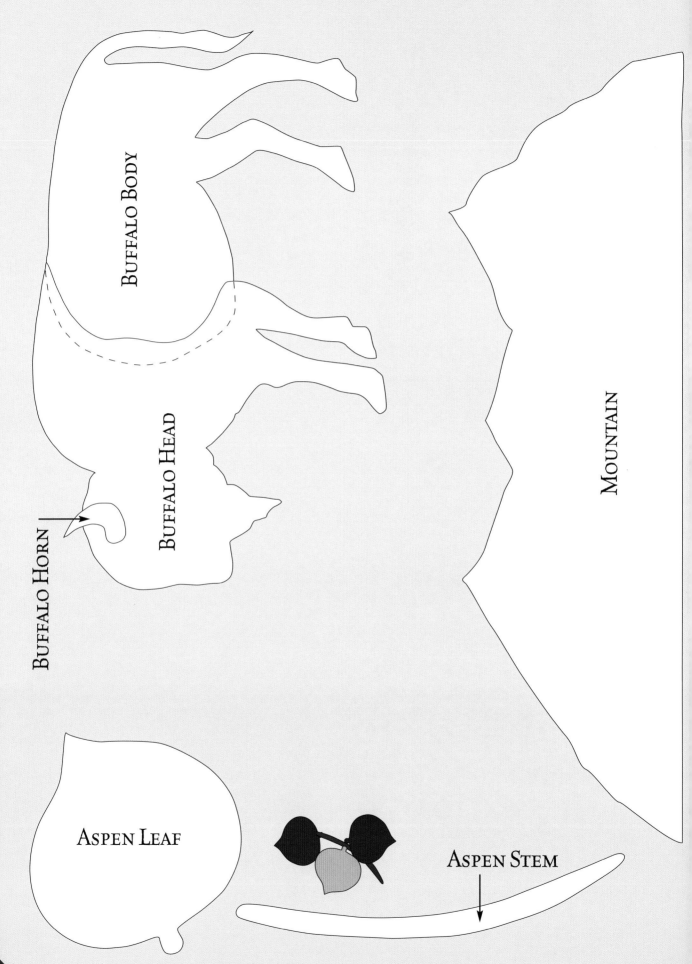

BUFFALO BODY

BUFFALO HEAD

BUFFALO HORN

MOUNTAIN

ASPEN LEAF

ASPEN STEM

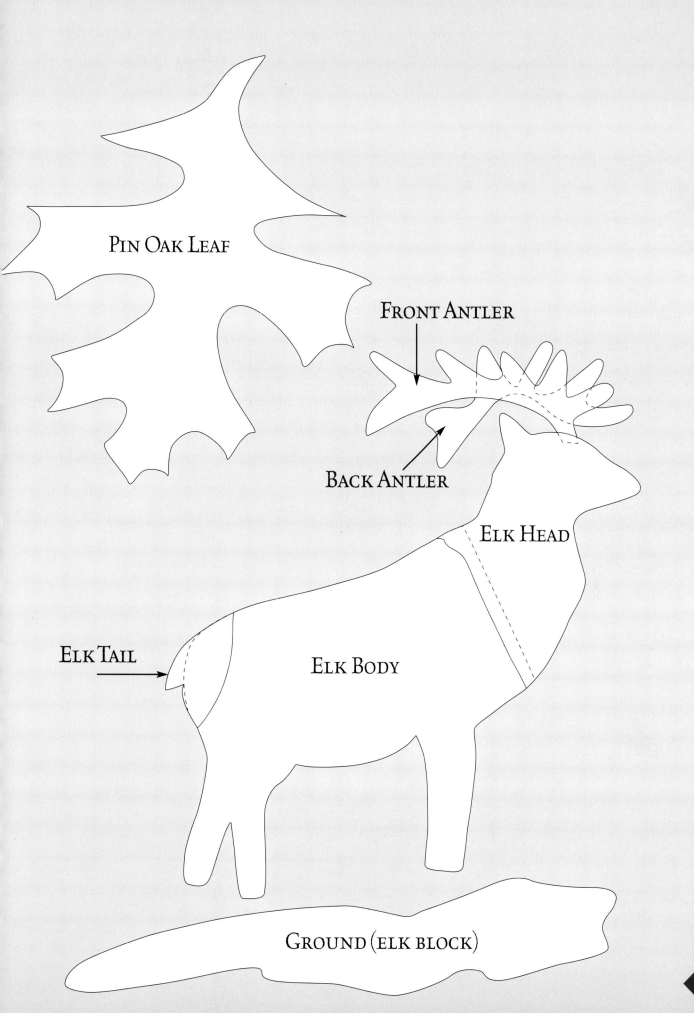

PIN OAK LEAF

FRONT ANTLER

BACK ANTLER

ELK HEAD

ELK TAIL

ELK BODY

GROUND (ELK BLOCK)

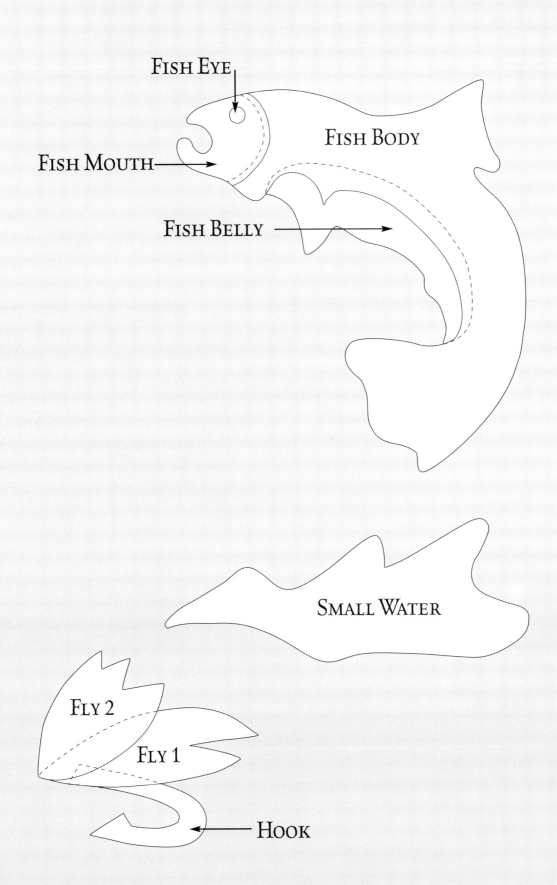

FISH EYE

FISH MOUTH

FISH BODY

FISH BELLY

SMALL WATER

FLY 2

FLY 1

HOOK

PINE SPRIG

PINE CONE

LARGE WATER

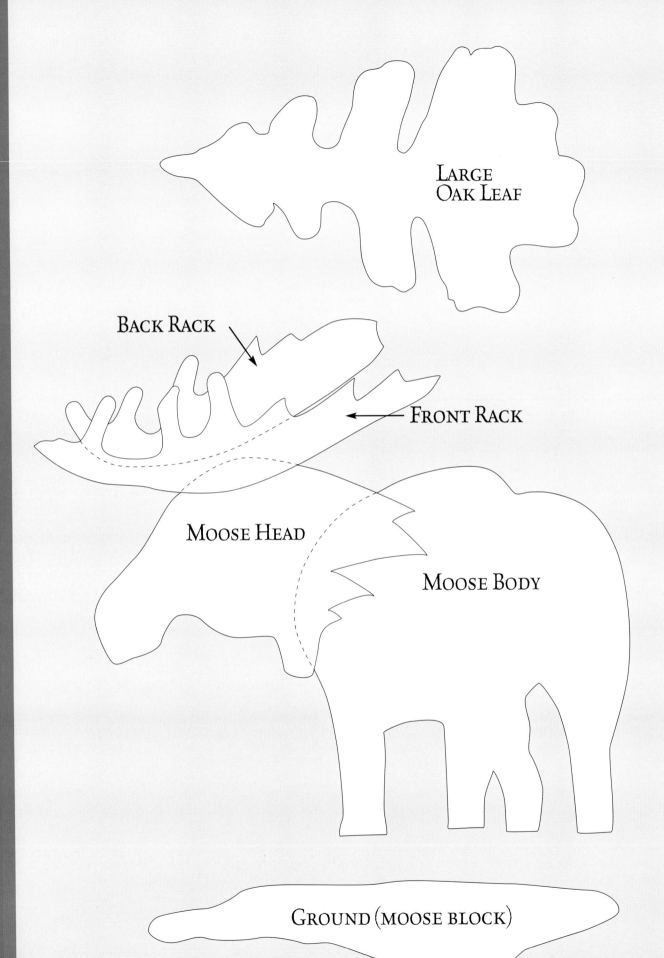

LARGE
OAK LEAF

BACK RACK

FRONT RACK

MOOSE HEAD

MOOSE BODY

GROUND (MOOSE BLOCK)

MOON

MAPLE LEAF

WOLF

GROUND (WOLVES BLOCK)

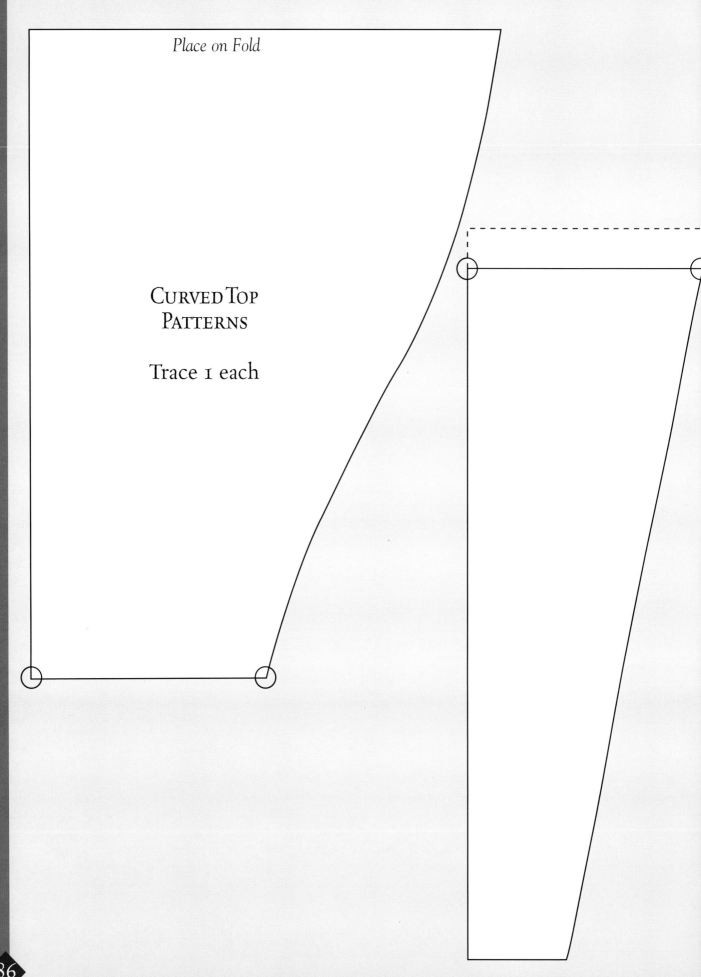

*Place on Fold*

CURVED TOP
PATTERNS

Trace 1 each

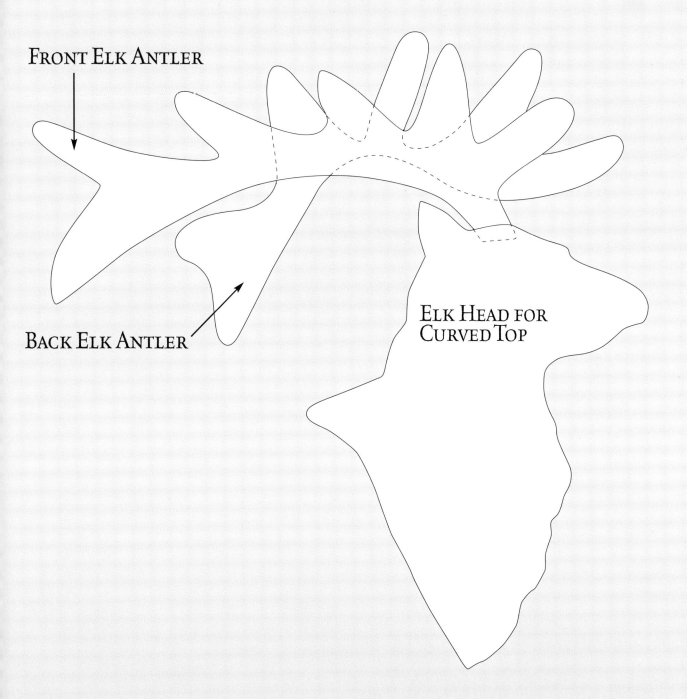

FRONT ELK ANTLER

BACK ELK ANTLER

ELK HEAD FOR
CURVED TOP

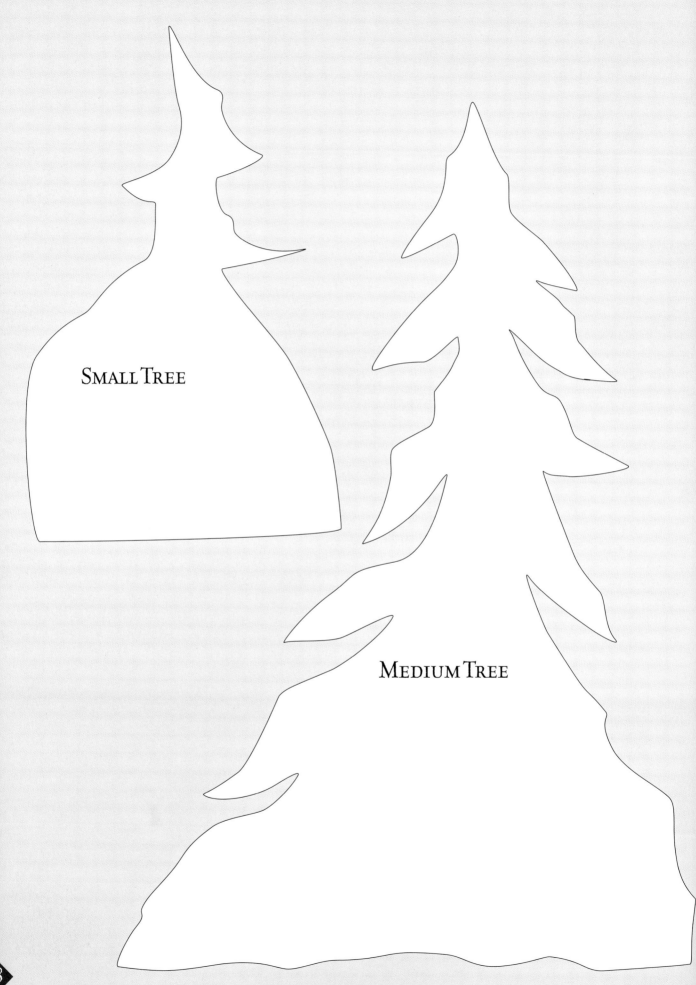

SMALL TREE

MEDIUM TREE

LARGE TREE

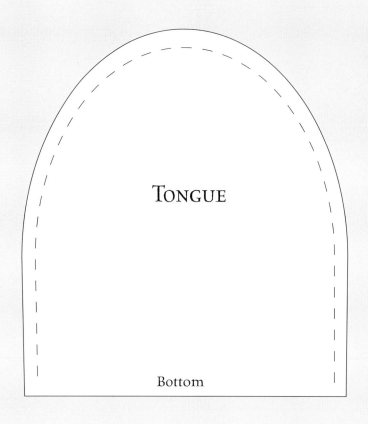

Tongue

Bottom

Large Oak Leaf

Small Oak Leaf

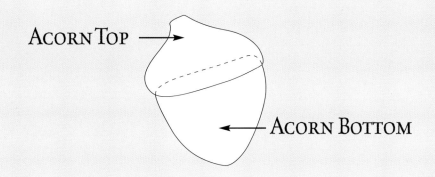

ACORN TOP

ACORN BOTTOM

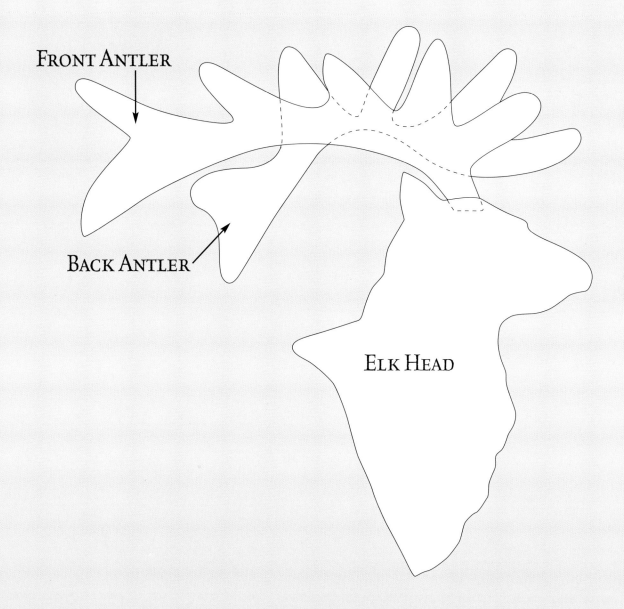

FRONT ANTLER

BACK ANTLER

ELK HEAD

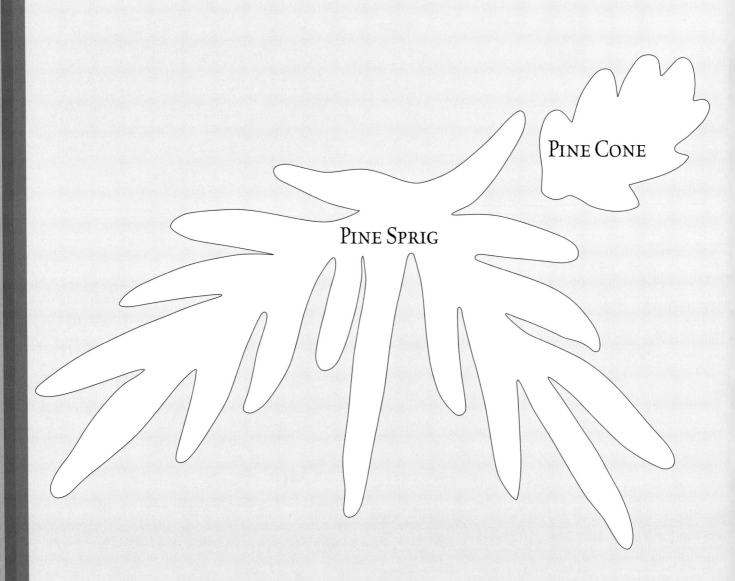

PINE CONE

PINE SPRIG

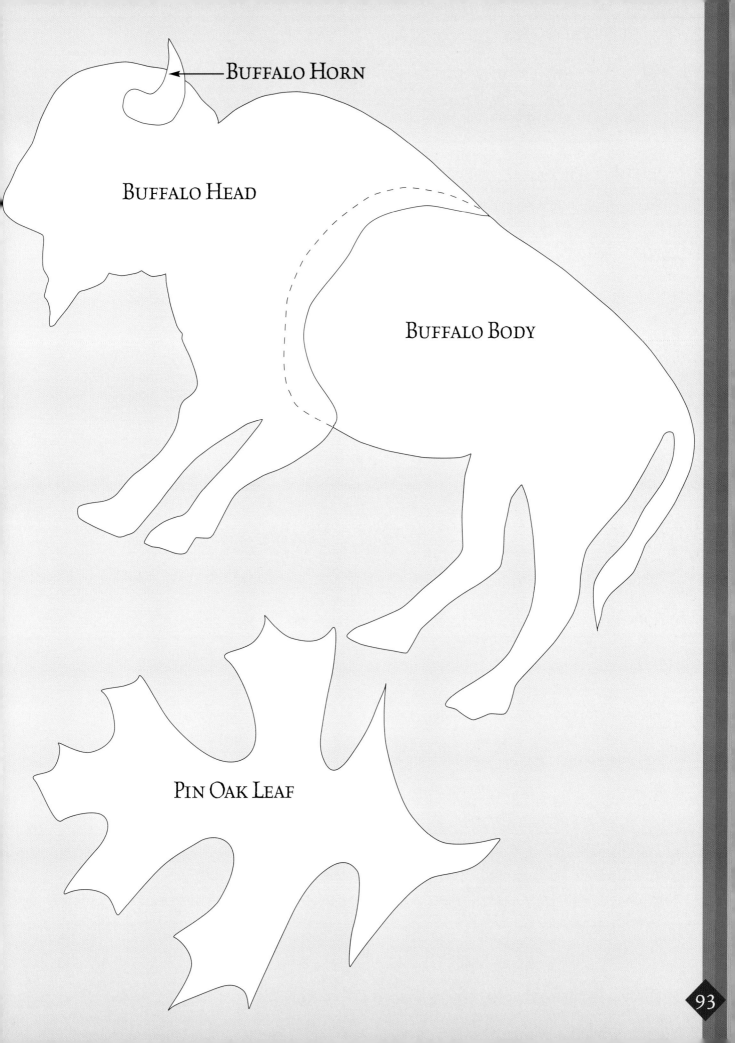

BUFFALO HORN

BUFFALO HEAD

BUFFALO BODY

PIN OAK LEAF

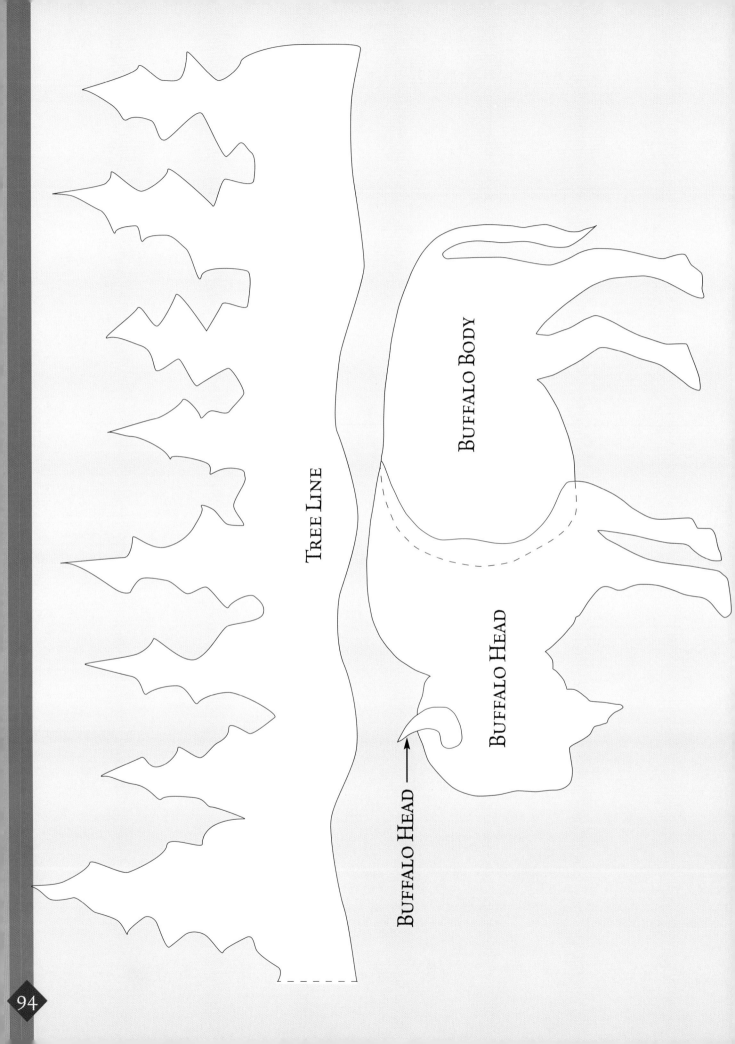

TREE LINE

BUFFALO BODY

BUFFALO HEAD

BUFFALO HEAD ⟶

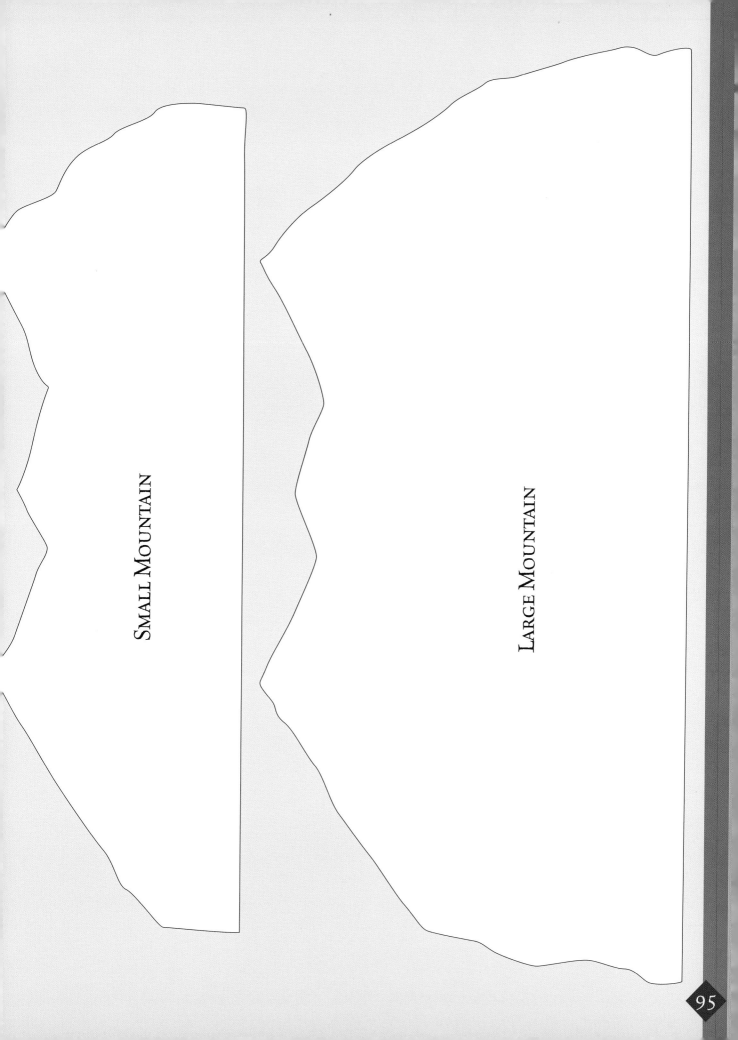

SMALL MOUNTAIN

LARGE MOUNTAIN

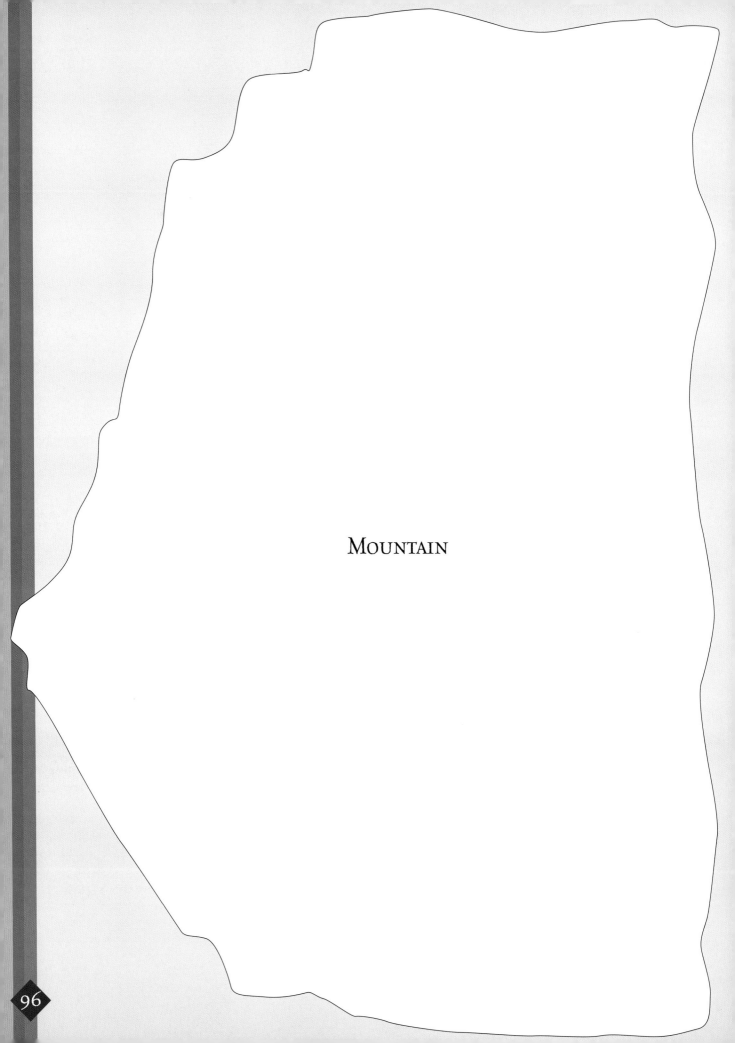

MOUNTAIN

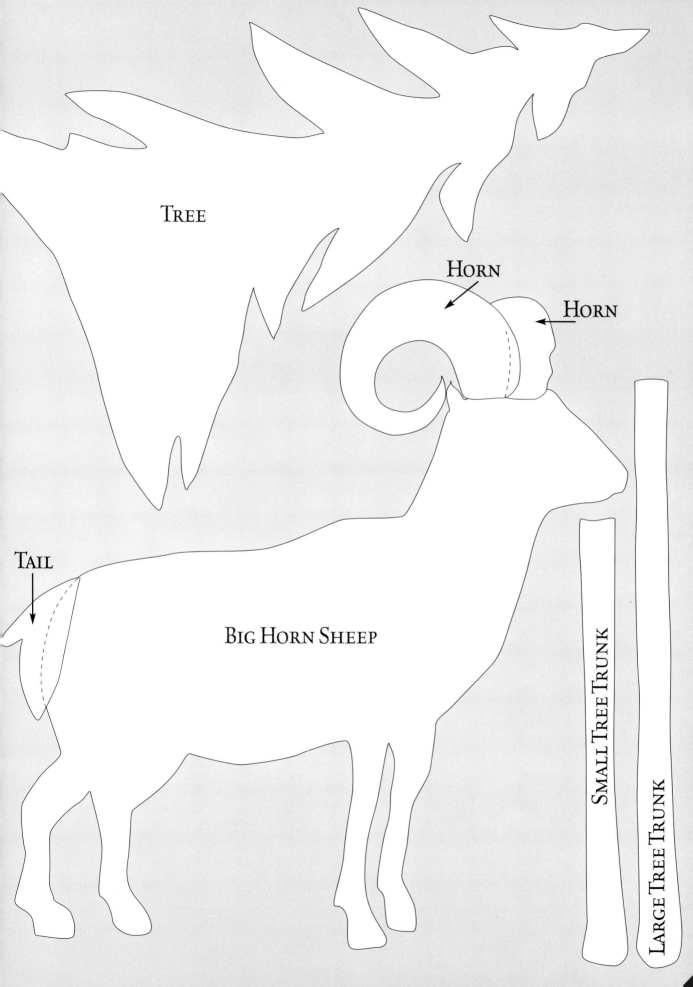

Tree

Horn

Horn

Tail

Big Horn Sheep

Small Tree Trunk

Large Tree Trunk

# Quilting the Lodge Look

## INTRODUCTION

Welcome to the lodge. Invite nature indoors with projects inspired by wildlife and the great outdoors.

On the following pages you'll find nine 21" x 21" patchwork quilt blocks inspired by traditional nature-themed block patterns such as Bear Paw, Flying Geese, Maple Leaf and Log Cabin—each with its own appliquéd scene celebrating wildlife and the great outdoors. You can assemble all nine blocks into a fabulous sampler quilt, MEMORIES FROM THE LODGE or choose four favorite blocks to make a wallhanging. The sampler quilt sets the scene for smaller projects using one or more of the wonderful wildlife appliqué scenes.

Choose from five bonus snuggler quilts—just the right size for comfortable evenings in front of the fire or watching a favorite movie.

Whether you start small by choosing a favorite small project or capture the essence of several blocks to create one spectacular wildlife habitat quilt or wallhanging, you're sure to enjoy quilting the lodge look.

## Debbie Field

# Memories From the Lodge
## Quilt

## Materials

*Finished size is approximately 84" x 84"*

Refer to the general instructions on pages 6-7
before starting this project.

*Fabrics are based on 42"-wide cotton
fabric that has not been washed.*

9 completed blocks

1/4 yard of brown fabric for the cornerstones

1 yard of tan fabric for sashing

2-3/4 yards of print for
the outer border and the binding

Queen size batting

8 yards of fabric for backing (seamed to fit)

## Cutting Instructions

*(A 1/4" seam allowance is included in these measurements.)*

• From the brown fabric, cut:
  1 strip 2-1/2" x 42"; from this strip, cut:
  16 squares 2-1/2" x 2-1/2"

• From the tan fabric, cut:
  12 strips 2-1/2" x 42"; from these strips, cut:
  24 rectangles 2-1/2" x 21-1/2" for sashing

• From the print fabric, cut:
  9 strips 6-1/2" x 42" for the outer border
  9 strips 3" x 42" for the binding

## Assembling the Quilt top

1. Sew groups of three blocks and four sashing strips together as shown. Press toward the sashing strips. You will have three rows total.

2. Sew four cornerstones and three sashing strips together as shown. Press toward the sashing strips. You will have four completed sashing strips.

3. Sew the rows and sashing strips together, as shown. Press toward the sashing strips.

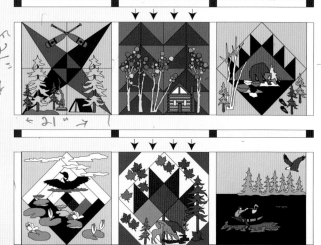

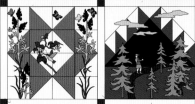

## Adding the Borders

1. Measure the width of the quilt top through the center to get top and bottom border measurement. Cut two strips to that measurement from the 6-1/2" print

border strips. Sew border strips to the top and bottom. Press toward the border.

2. Measure the length of the quilt top through the center to get side border measurement. Cut two strips to that measurement from the 6-1/2" print border strips. Sew the border strips to each side. Press toward the border.

## Finishing the Quilt

1. Layer the quilt backing fabric, batting, and quilt top. Baste the layers together.

2. Hand or machine quilt as desired.

3. Finish the quilt by sewing on the binding.

# 4-Block Wallhanging

## Materials

*Finished size is approximately 54" x 54"*

Refer to the general instructions on pages 6-7 before starting this project.

*Fabrics are based on 42"-wide cotton fabric that has not been washed.*

4 completed blocks

■

1/8 yard of dark red fabric for the cornerstones

■

5/8 yard of cream fabric for sashing

■

1-1/2 yards of dark teal fabric for the outer border and the binding

■

60" x 60" piece of batting

■

3-1/2 yards of fabric for backing (seamed to fit)

## Cutting Instructions

- From the dark red fabric, cut:
  1 strip 2-1/2" x 42"; from this strip, cut:
    9 squares 2-1/2" x 2-1/2" for cornerstones

- From the cream fabric, cut:
  7 strips 2-1/2" x 42"; from these strips, cut:
    12 rectangles 2-1/2" x 21-1/2" for sashing

- From the dark teal fabric, cut:
  6 strips 4-1/2" x 42" for border
  6 strips 2-3/4" x 42" for binding

## Assembling the Wallhanging

1. Sew groups of two blocks and three sashing strips together, as shown. Press toward the sashing strips. You will have two rows total.

2. Sew three cornerstones and two sashing strips together, as shown. Press toward the sashing strips. You will have three completed sashing strips.

3. Sew the rows and sashing strips together, as shown. Press toward the sashing strips.

## Adding the Borders

1. Measure the width of the quilt top through the center to get top and bottom border measurement. Cut two strips to that measurement from the 4-1/2" dark teal border strips. Sew border strips to the top and bottom. Press toward the border.

2. Measure the length of the quilt top through the center to get side border measurement. Cut two strips to that measurement. Press toward the outside.

## Finishing the Wallhanging

1. Layer quilt backing fabric, batting, and top.

2. Quilt and bind.

# CROSSED CANOES BLOCK

The traditional Crossed Canoes block takes you on a portaging
adventure with patterns for everything from campsite to
canoes to appliqué on a 4-block snuggler, pillow, and place mats.

## Materials

*Finished size is approximately 21" x 21"*

Refer to the general instructions on pages 6-7 before starting this project.

*Fabrics are based on 42"-wide cotton fabric that has not been washed.*

3/4 yard of light tan fabric for background

1/4 yard of dark red fabric for canoes

1/4 yard of dark green fabric for canoes

1/4 yard total of 2 shades of green fabric for trees

Scraps of light and dark blue fabric for tent, water

Scraps of brown fabric for logs in campfire, tent pole, and tree trunks

Scrap of gray fabric for smoke

Scrap of red fabric for flame

Scrap of gold fabric for canoe paddles

Scraps of red, black, and blue fabric for trim on paddles

1 yard of fusible web

Stabilizer for appliqués

Sulky® threads to match appliqué fabrics

## Crossed Canoes Block

### Cutting Instructions

*(A 1/4" seam allowance is included in these measurements.)*

- From the light tan fabric, cut:
  2 strips 11" x 42"; from these strips, cut:
      4 squares 11" x 11"

- From the dark red fabric, cut:
  1 strip 3-1/2" x 42"; from this strip, cut:
      2 squares 3-1/2" x 3-1/2"

- From the dark green fabric, cut:
  1 strip 3-1/2" x 42"; from this strip, cut:
      2 squares 3-1/2" x 3-1/2"

## Assembling the Block

1. Diagonally mark the wrong side of the dark red and dark green 3-1/2" squares.

2. Place a dark red 3-1/2" square on a corner of an 11" light tan square. Sew on the marked diagonal line. Trim seam allowance to 1/4" and press. You will need 2 Unit A.

*Unit A; Make 2*

3. Repeat step 2, using the dark green 3-1/2" squares. You will need 2 Unit B.

*Unit B; Make 2*

## Adding the Appliqués

1. Trace all appliqué templates from pages 108-111 and cut them out.

2. Refer to general instructions to prepare pieces for appliqué.

3. Use lightweight tear-away stabilizer to machine appliqué the pieces. Place the stabilizer beneath the fabric layers and use a small zigzag stitch to sew around each shape, smoothly covering the raw fabric edge. If your machine has stitch options, use them to detail the appliqués. After the stitching is complete, remove the stabilizer according to the manufacturer's instructions.

4. On the Unit A background squares, appliqué a dark green canoe point to the dark red triangle to make 1 Unit A. You will need 2 Unit A.

5. On the Unit B background squares, appliqué a dark red canoe point to the dark green triangle to make 1 Unit B. You will need 2 Unit B.

6. Sew a Unit A and a Unit B together to make 1 Unit C. Press toward Unit A. You will need 2 Unit C.

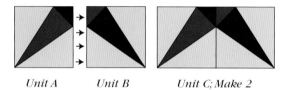

*Unit A*          *Unit B*          *Unit C; Make 2*

7. Sew two Unit C together to make 1 Unit D. Press in the direction of least amount of bulk.

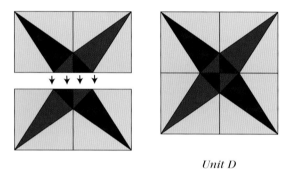

*Unit D*

8. Refer to the diagram below and on page 106 to position the appliqué pieces on the block. Stitch around the appliqué pieces with a small zigzag stitch to finish rough edges.

## Templates for Crossed Canoes Block

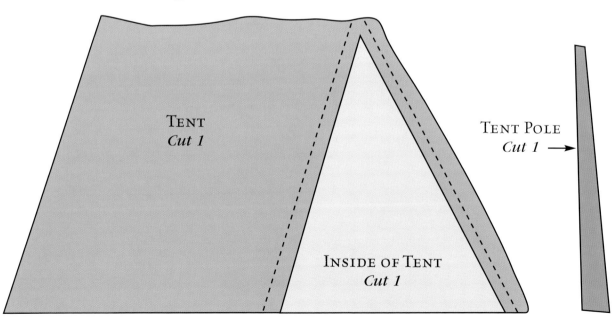

TENT
*Cut 1*

INSIDE OF TENT
*Cut 1*

TENT POLE
*Cut 1* →

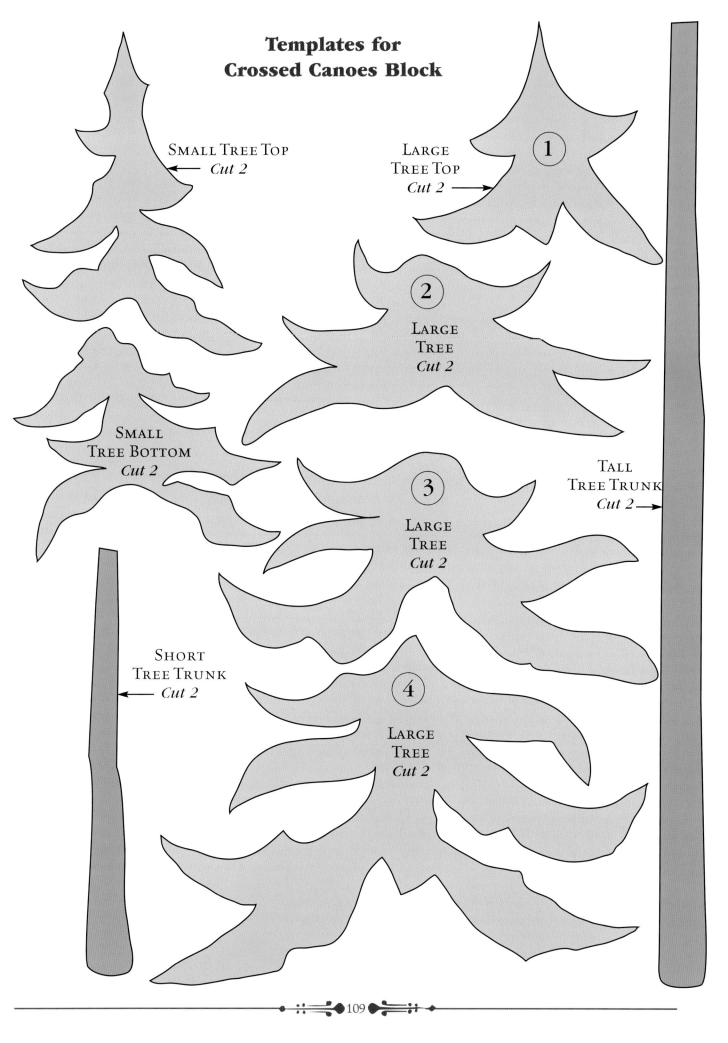

# Templates for Crossed Canoes Block

SMALL TREE TOP
*Cut 2*

LARGE
TREE TOP
*Cut 2*

①

②
LARGE
TREE
*Cut 2*

SMALL
TREE BOTTOM
*Cut 2*

③
LARGE
TREE
*Cut 2*

TALL
TREE TRUNK
*Cut 2*

SHORT
TREE TRUNK
*Cut 2*

④
LARGE
TREE
*Cut 2*

# Templates for Crossed Canoes Block

**B**

**CANOE POINT A**
*Cut 2 Dark Green*
*Cut 2 Dark Red*

Match the dotted
circles to make
one piece

**CANOE POINT B**
*Cut 2 Dark Green*
*Cut 2 Dark Red*

Match the dotted
circles to make
one piece

**A**

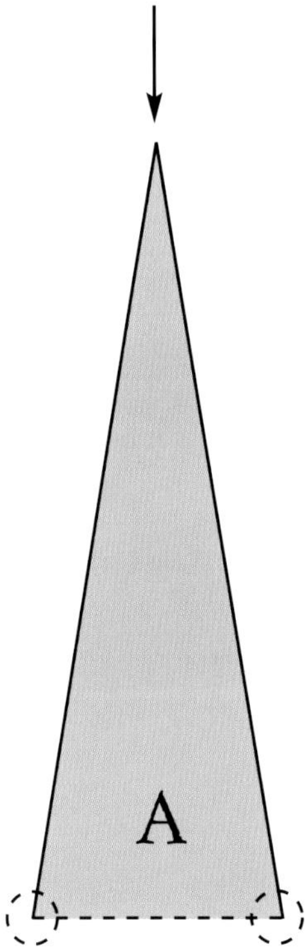

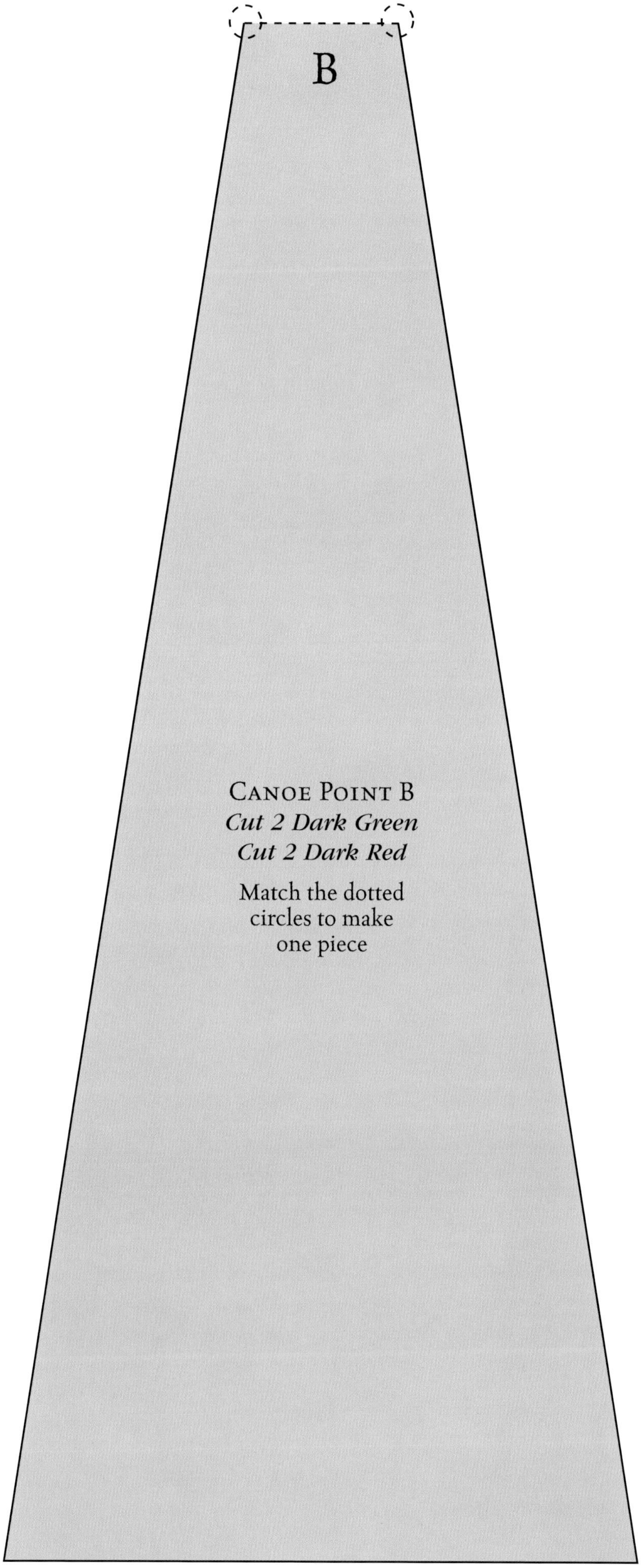

# Templates for Crossed Canoes Block

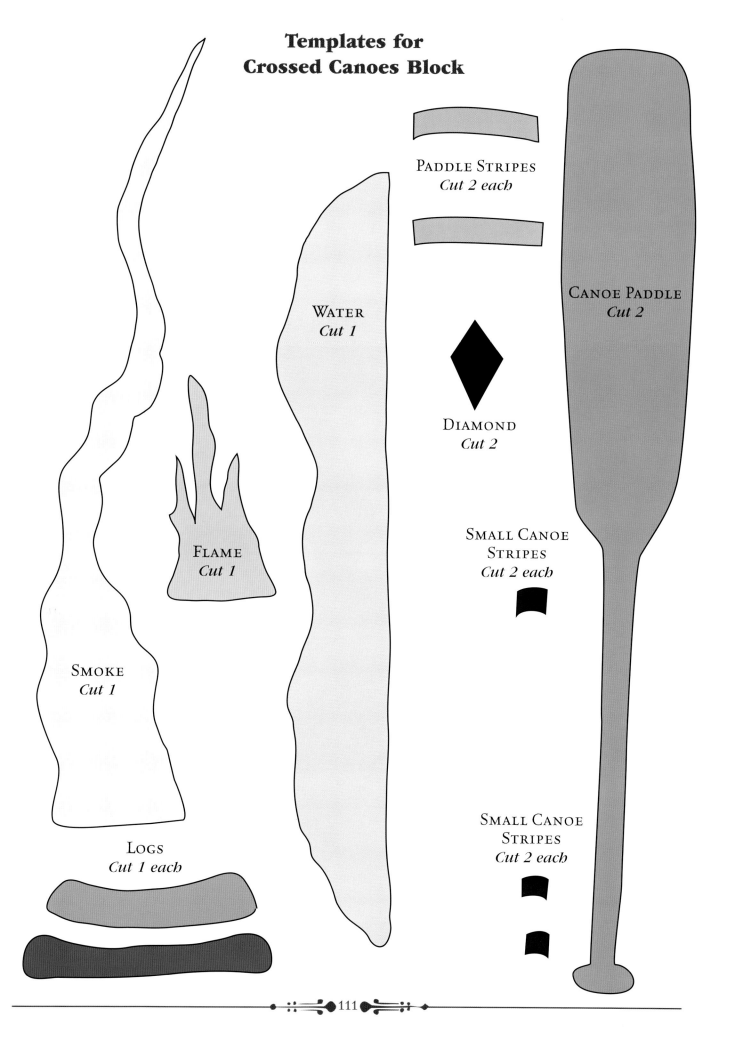

PADDLE STRIPES
*Cut 2 each*

WATER
*Cut 1*

CANOE PADDLE
*Cut 2*

DIAMOND
*Cut 2*

FLAME
*Cut 1*

SMALL CANOE
STRIPES
*Cut 2 each*

SMOKE
*Cut 1*

SMALL CANOE
STRIPES
*Cut 2 each*

LOGS
*Cut 1 each*

# CANOE SNUGGLER

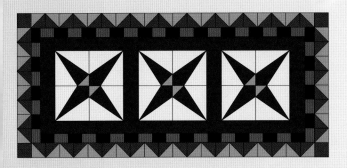

## Materials

***Finished size is approximately 72" x 72"***

Refer to the general instructions on pages 6-7 before starting this project.

***Fabrics are based on 40"-wide flannel fabric that has not been washed.***

2 yards of tan flannel for background

■

3 yards of dark dark red flannel for canoe points, sashing, outside border, and binding

■

1/2 yard of brown flannel for checkered border

■

1/2 yard of black flannel for checkered border

■

7/8 yard of gold flannel for canoe centers and triangle border

■

7/8 yard of green flannel for triangle border

■

1-3/4 yards of fusible web

■

82" x 82" piece of batting

■

5 yards of flannel for backing

■

Sulky® threads to match canoe appliqués

## Canoe Blocks

Make 4

### Cutting Instructions

*(A 1/4" seam allowance is included in measurements.)*

• From the tan flannel, cut:
  6 strips 10-1/2" x 40"; from these strips, cut:
    16 squares 10-1/2" x 10-1/2"

• From the dark red flannel, cut:
  1 strip 3-1/2" x 40"; from this strip, cut:
    8 squares 3-1/2" x 3-1/2"
  13 strips 4-1/2" x 40" for sashing and outside border
  8 strips 3" x 40" for binding

• From the brown flannel, cut:
  4 strips 2-1/2" x 40"; from these strips, cut:
    27 rectangles 2-1/2" x 4-1/2"

• From the black flannel, cut:
  4 strips 2-1/2" x 40"; from these strips, cut:
    27 rectangles 2-1/2" x 4-1/2"

• From the gold flannel, cut:
  1 strip 3-1/2" x 40"; from this strip, cut:
    8 squares 3-1/2" x 3-1/2"
  4 strips 4-7/8" x 40"; from these strips, cut:
    28 squares 4-7/8" x 4-7/8"; cut squares in half
    diagonally to make 56 half-square triangles.

• From the green flannel, cut:
  1 strip 4-1/2" x 40"; from this strip, cut:
    4 squares 4-1/2" x 4-1/2"
  4 strips 4-7/8" x 40"; from these strips, cut:
    28 squares 4-7/8" x 4-7/8"; cut squares in half
    diagonally to make 56 half-square triangles.

## Assembling the Blocks

1. Draw a diagonal line on the back of the 8 gold 3-1/2" x 3-1/2" squares and the 8 dark red 3-1/2" x 3-1/2" squares.

2. Place a dark red 3-1/2" square on a corner of a 10-1/2" tan square. Sew on the marked diagonal line. Trim seam allowance to 1/4" and press. You will need 8 Unit A.

*Unit A; Make 8*

3. Repeat step 2, using the gold 3-1/2" squares. You will need 8 Unit B.

*Unit B; Make 8*

## Appliquéing the Canoes to the Blocks

1. Trace canoe point appliqué from page 110 and cut out.

2. Trace 16 canoe points onto fusible web. Fuse to dark red. Cut out the points and position them on the tan squares. Refer to diagram on page 116 for placement. Stitch around appliqués with a small zigzag stitch.

3. Sew a Unit A and a Unit B together, as shown to make 1 Unit C. Press toward Unit A. You will need 8 Unit C.

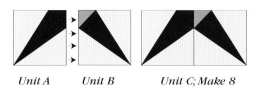

*Unit A*    *Unit B*    *Unit C; Make 8*

4. Sew 2 Unit C together to make 1 Unit D. Press in the direction of least amount of bulk. You will need 4 Unit D. The canoe blocks should measure 20-1/2" to each unfinished edge.

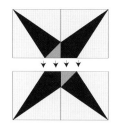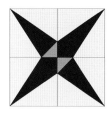

*Unit D; Make 4*

## Adding the Sashing and Inner Borders

1. Cut 2 dark red 20-1/2" sashing rectangles from the dark red 4-1/2" x 40" strips.

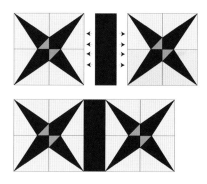

2. Sew the sashing rectangles between 2 Unit D. Press toward the sashing. You will need 2 rows.

3. Seaming as needed, cut 3 dark red 44-1/2" sashing strips from the dark red 4-1/2" x 40" strips.

4. Sew the strips and rows together. Press toward the sashing strips.

5. Seaming the strips as needed, cut 2 dark red strips 52-1/2" from the dark red 4-1/2" x 40" strips. Sew to each side of quilt top and press toward the sashing.

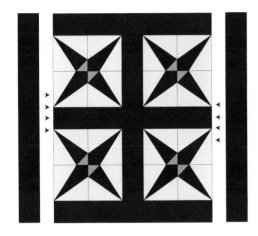

6. Using 13 brown 2-1/2" x 4-1/2" rectangles and 13 black 2-1/2" x 4-1/2" rectangles make 2 checkered borders for the top and bottom. Press. For the bottom border use 6 brown 2-1/2" x 4-1/2" rectangles and 7 black 2-1/2" x 4-1/2" rectangles. For the top border use 7 brown 2-1/2" x 4-1/2" rectangles and 6 black 2-1/2" x 4-1/2" rectangles.

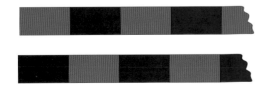

7. Sew the rows to the top and bottom of the quilt top. Press toward the border.

8. Using 14 brown 2-1/2" x 4-1/2" rectangles and 14 black 2-1/2" x 4-1/2" rectangles make two borders for the sides. Press. Use 7 brown 2-1/2" x 4-1/2" rectangles and 7 black 2-1/2" x 4-1/2" rectangles for each side border.

9. For the triangle border, sew a gold 4-7/8" half-square triangle and a green 4-7/8" half-square triangle together to make 1 Unit E. Press toward the green. You will need 56 Unit E.

*Unit E; Make 56*

10. Sew 2 Unit E together to make 1 Unit F. Press in the direction of least amount of bulk. You will need 28 Unit F for the triangle border.

*Unit F; Make 28*

11. Sew 7 Unit F together to make 1 Unit G. Press in the direction of least amount of bulk. You will need 4 rows of Unit G.

*Unit G; Make 4*

12. Sew a green 4-1/2" square on each end of Unit G to make Unit H. Press toward the green. You will need 2 Unit H.

*Unit H; Make 2*

13. Sew a Unit G on the top and bottom of the quilt top. Press toward the triangle border.

14. Sew a Unit H on each side of the quilt top. Press toward the triangle border.

## Adding the Outer Borders

1. Measure the width of the the quilt top through the center to get the top and bottom outside border measurement. Cut 2 border strips to that length from the dark red 4-1/2" x 40" strips. Sew the border strips to the top and bottom of quilt. Press toward the border.

2. Measure the length of the quilt top through the center to get side border measurements. Cut 2 border strips that length from the dark red 4-1/2" x 40" strips. Sew to each side of the quilt. Press toward the border.

## Finishing the Quilt

1. Layer the quilt backing fabric, the batting, and the quilt top. Baste the layers together.

2. Hand or machine quilt as desired.

3. Finish the quilt by sewing on the binding.

## Canoe Snuggler

# Quilt it Quick

# Crossed Canoes Pillow

## Materials

*Finished size is approximately 17" x 17"*

Refer to the general instructions on pages 6-7 before starting this project.

*Fabrics are based on 42"-wide cotton fabric that has not been washed.*

3/8 yard of cream fabric for pillow center

∎

1/8 yard of dark green fabric for inner border

∎

1 yard of dark red fabric for outer border and pillow back

∎

Scraps of dark red, green, brown, gold, blue, and black fabric for appliqués

∎

16" x 16" pillow form

∎

20" x 20" square of batting

∎

3/4 yard of fusible web

∎

Sulky® threads to match appliqué fabrics

## Cutting Instructions

• From the cream fabric, cut:
  12" x 12" square

• From the dark green fabric, cut:
  2 strips 1-3/4" x 42" for inner border

• From the dark red fabric, cut:
  2 strips 2-1/4" x 42" for the outer border

## Assembling the Pillow

1. Trace all appliqué templates from pages 118-119 and cut them out.

2. Refer to general instructions to prepare pieces for appliqué.

3. Arrange appliqué pieces onto the cream 12" x 12" square. Refer to photo for appliqué placement. Stitch around appliqués with a small zigzag stitch.

4. For the inner border, measure the width of the pillow top through the center to get the top and bottom measurement. Cut 2 border strips to that length from the dark green 1-3/4" x 42" strips. Sew to the top and bottom of the pillow. Press toward the outside. Measure the length of the pillow through the center and cut 2 strips to that length from the dark green 1-3/4" x 42" strips. Sew to the sides of pillow.

5. For the outer border, measure the width of the pillow top through the center for the top and bottom measurement. Cut 2 border strips that length from the dark red 2-1/4" x 42" strips. Sew to the top and bottom of the pillow. Press toward the outside. Measure the length of the pillow through the center and cut 2 strips that length from the dark red 2-1/4" x 42" strips. Sew to the sides of the pillow.

## Finishing the Pillow

1. Layer batting and pillow top. Quilt as desired.

2. Press and trim excess batting from pillow top. Layer backing (right side up) and pillow top wrong side up. Stitch 1/4" seam around pillow top, leaving bottom open to insert pillow form or fiberfill. Clip corners and trim away any excess backing fabric.

3. Turn to right side. Insert pillow form and stitch opening closed.

# CANOE RENTAL

**Placement Diagram**

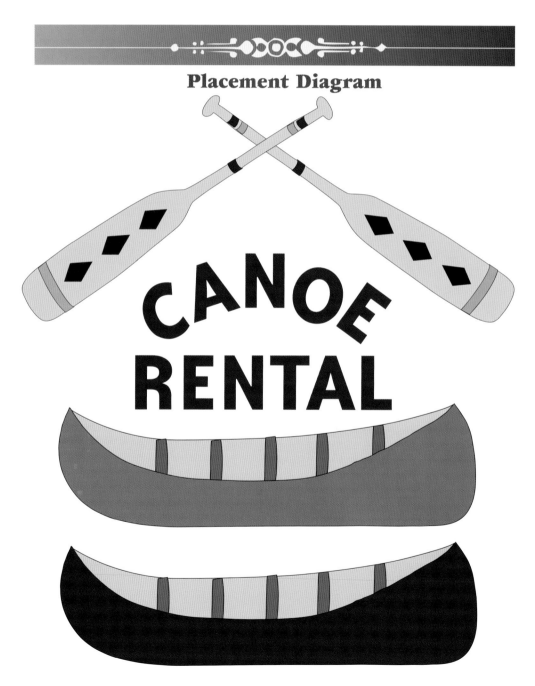

CANOE RENTAL

# Templates for Canoe Rental Pillow

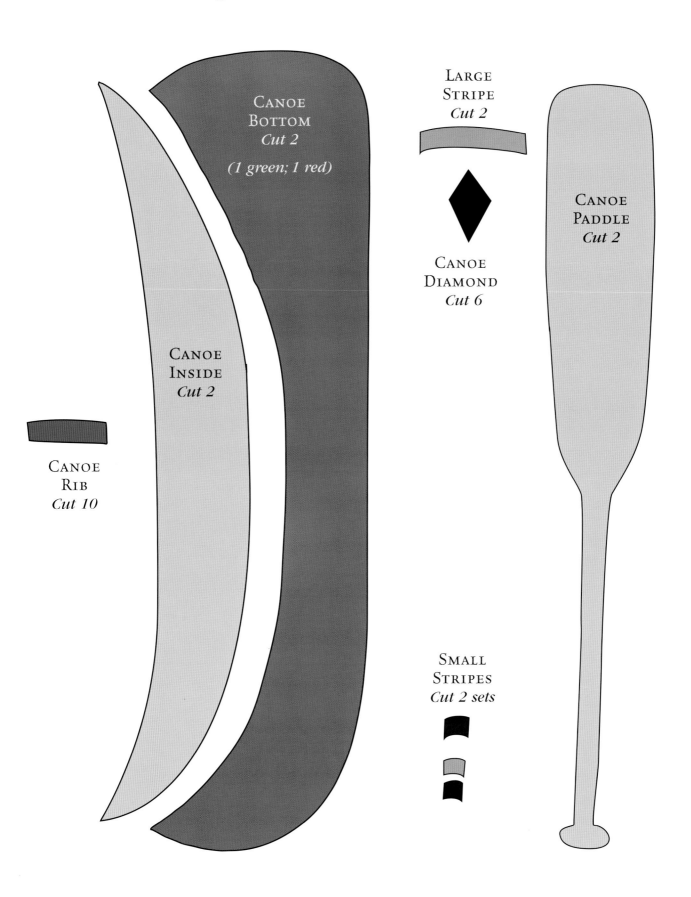

CANOE
BOTTOM
*Cut 2*

*(1 green; 1 red)*

LARGE
STRIPE
*Cut 2*

CANOE
DIAMOND
*Cut 6*

CANOE
PADDLE
*Cut 2*

CANOE
INSIDE
*Cut 2*

CANOE
RIB
*Cut 10*

SMALL
STRIPES
*Cut 2 sets*

# Quilt it Quick

# Crossed Canoes
# Table Setting

## Materials

*Finished size is approximately 13" x 19"*

Refer to the general instructions on pages 6-7
before starting this project.

*Fabrics are based on 42"-wide cotton
fabric that has not been washed.
Yardage listed is enough for four place mats.*

1/2 yard cream fabric for centers

■

3/4 yard of dark red fabric
for border and backing

■

Scraps of gold fabric for canoe paddles

■

3/4 yard of black fabric for binding

■

Scraps of red, black, and blue fabric
for paddle trims

■

34" x 46" piece of batting

■

1-5/8 yard fabric for backing

■

14" x 14" piece of fusible web for each place mat

■

Stabilizer for appliqués

■

Sulky® threads to match appliqué fabrics

## Place Mats

### Cutting Instructions

*(A 1/4" seam allowance is included in these measurements.)*

• From the cream fabric, cut:
  1 strip 13-1/2" x 42"; from this strip cut:
    4 rectangles 13-1/2" x 7-1/2"

• From the dark red fabric, cut:
  6 strips 3-1/2" x 42"; from these strips cut:
    16 rectangles 3-1/2" x 13-1/2"

• From the black fabric, cut:
  7 strips 2-1/2" x 42" for binding

### Assembling the Place Mats

1.  Sew a dark red 3-1/2" x 13-1/2" rectangle to the
    top and bottom of each cream 13-1/2" x 7-1/2"
    rectangle. Press toward the dark red rectangle.

2.  Sew a dark red 3-1/2" x 13-1/2" rectangle to the sides
    of each rectangle from Step 1. Press toward the dark
    red rectangle.

3.  Trace and cut out all appliqué templates from
    page 121.

4.  Refer to general instructions to prepare pieces
    for appliqué.

5.  Use lightweight tear-away stabilizer to machine

appliqué. Place the stabilizer beneath the fabric layers and use a small zigzag stitch to sew around each shape, smoothly covering the raw fabric edge. If your machine has stitch options, use them to detail appliqués. After the stitching is complete, remove the stabilizer according to the manufacturer's instructions.

## Finishing the Place Mats

1. Layer the backing fabric, batting, and place mat top. Baste the layers together.

2. Hand or machine quilt as desired.

3. Finish the place mats by sewing on the binding.

## Napkins

### Materials

*Finished size is approximately 17" x 17"*

*Fabrics are based on 42"-wide cotton fabric that has not been washed. Yardage listed is enough for four napkins.*

1-1/8" yards of cream fabric

## Cutting Instructions

*(A 1/4" seam allowance is included in these measurements.)*

• From the cream fabric, cut:
  4 squares 18" x 18"

## Finishing the Napkins

Sew a narrow, double hem around all four sides of the 4 squares.

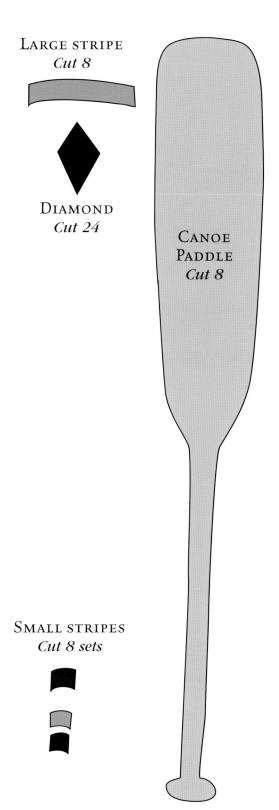

**Templates for Crossed Canoes Place Mats**

LARGE STRIPE
*Cut 8*

DIAMOND
*Cut 24*

CANOE PADDLE
*Cut 8*

SMALL STRIPES
*Cut 8 sets*

# FLYING GEESE BLOCK

An all-time favorite, the Flying Geese block is featured in a
12-block snuggler with appliqué patterns for an
outback cabin and aspen trees for a wilderness wallhanging.

## Materials

**Finished size is approximately 21" x 21"**

Refer to the general instructions on pages 6-7 before starting this project.

**Fabrics are based on 42"-wide cotton fabric that has not been washed.**

1/2 yard of purple fabric for background

1/2 yard of green fabric for background

1/2 yard of off-white fabric for aspen trees, cabin, left cabin roof, and right cabin roof

Assorted shades of gold fabric for aspen leaves

Scraps of yellow fabric for windows

Scraps of light brown fabric for logs, cabin roof, and cabin edge strip

Scraps of dark brown fabric for chimney and door

1 yard of fusible web

Stabilizer for appliqués

Sulky® threads to match appliqué fabrics

# Flying Geese Block

## Cutting Instructions

*(A 1/4" seam allowance is included in these measurements.)*

• From the purple fabric, cut:
  2 strips 6-1/8" x 42"; from these strips, cut:
      8 squares 6-1/8" x 6-1/8"; cut these squares in half diagonally to make 16 half-square triangles

• From the green fabric, cut:
  2 strips 6-1/8" x 42"; from these strips, cut:
      8 squares 6-1/8" x 6-1/8"; cut these squares in half diagonally to make 16 half-square triangles

## Assembling the Block

1. Sew the purple 6-1/8" half-square triangles and the green 6-1/8" half-square triangles together to make 1 Unit A. Press toward the green. You will need 16 Unit A.

*Unit A; Make 16*

2. Sew 2 Unit A together to make 1 Unit B. Press in the direction of least amount of bulk. You will need 8 Unit B.

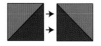 

*Unit B; Make 8*

3. Sew 2 Unit B together to make 1 Unit C. Press in the direction of least amount of bulk. You will need 4 Unit C.

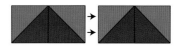 

*Unit C; Make 4*

4. Sew 4 Unit C together. Press in the direction of least amount of bulk.

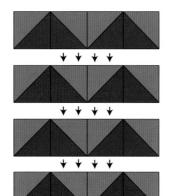 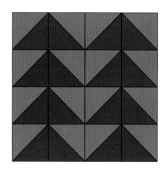

5. Trace all appliqué templates from pages 124-127 and cut out.

6. Refer to general instructions to prepare pieces for appliqué.

7. Use lightweight tear-away stabilizer to machine appliqué the pieces. Place the stabilizer beneath the fabric layers and use a small zigzag stitch to sew around each shape, smoothly covering the raw fabric edge. If your machine has stitch options, use them to detail the appliqués. After the stitching is complete, remove the stabilizer according to the manufacturer's instructions.

8. Refer to diagram on page 122 and at right to position appliqué pieces on the block. Stitch around the appliqué pieces with a small zigzag stitch to finish rough edges.

## Templates for Flying Geese Block

### ASPEN TREE
### *Cut 1*

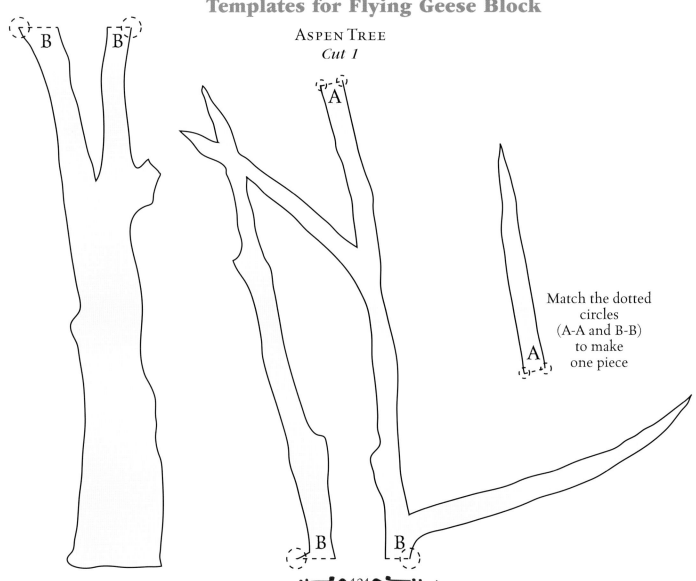

Match the dotted circles (A-A and B-B) to make one piece

# Templates for Flying Geese Block

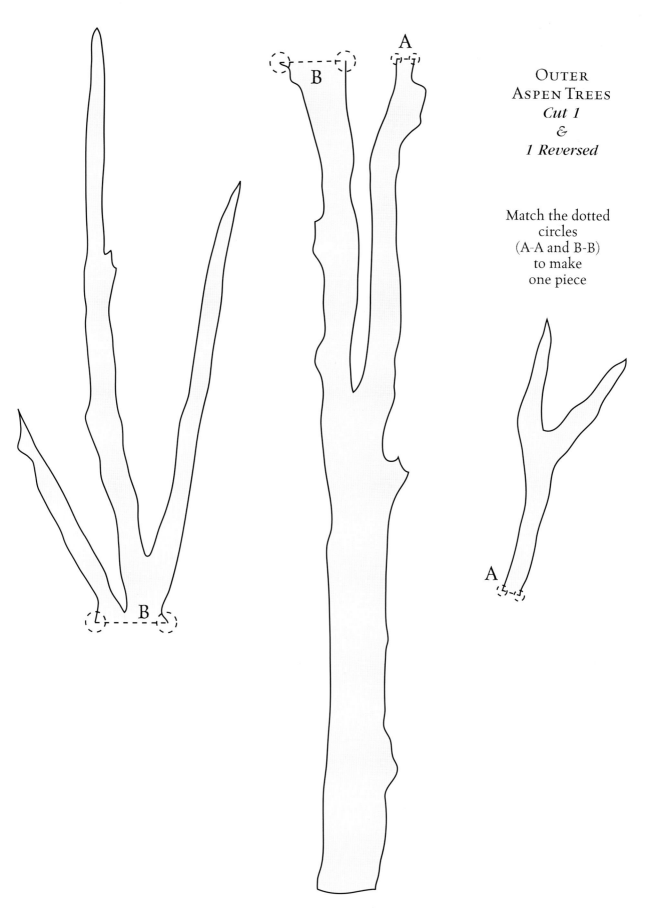

OUTER
ASPEN TREES
*Cut 1*
*&*
*1 Reversed*

Match the dotted
circles
(A-A and B-B)
to make
one piece

A

B

B

A

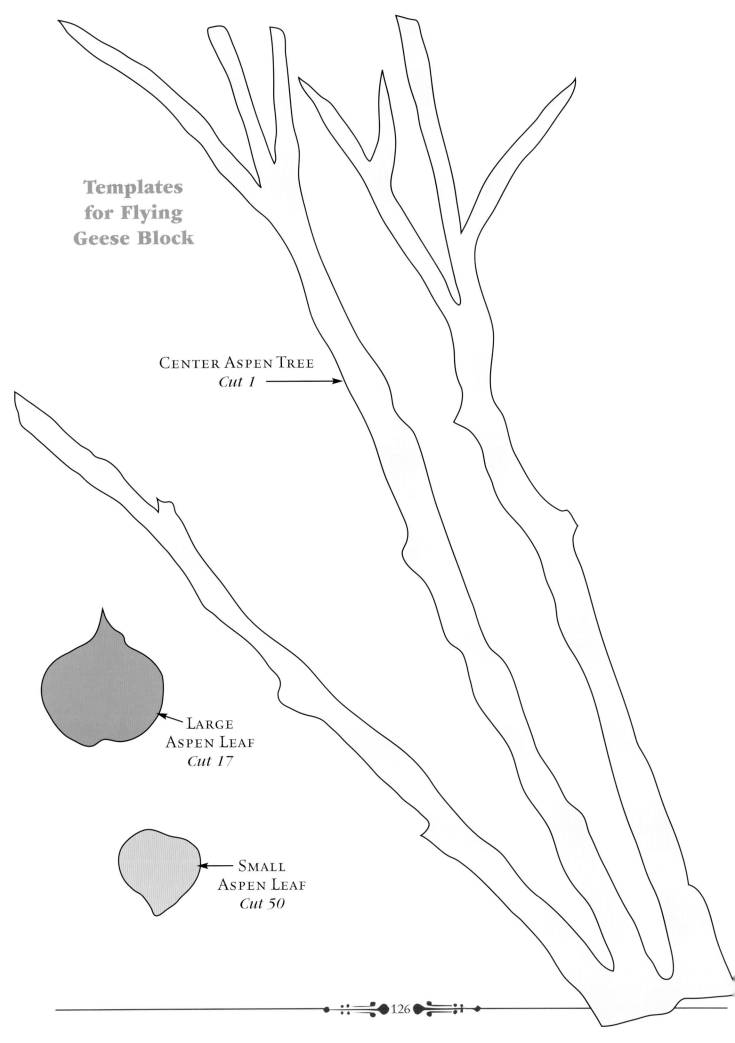

**Templates
for Flying
Geese Block**

CENTER ASPEN TREE
*Cut 1*

LARGE
ASPEN LEAF
*Cut 17*

SMALL
ASPEN LEAF
*Cut 50*

# Templates for Flying Geese Block

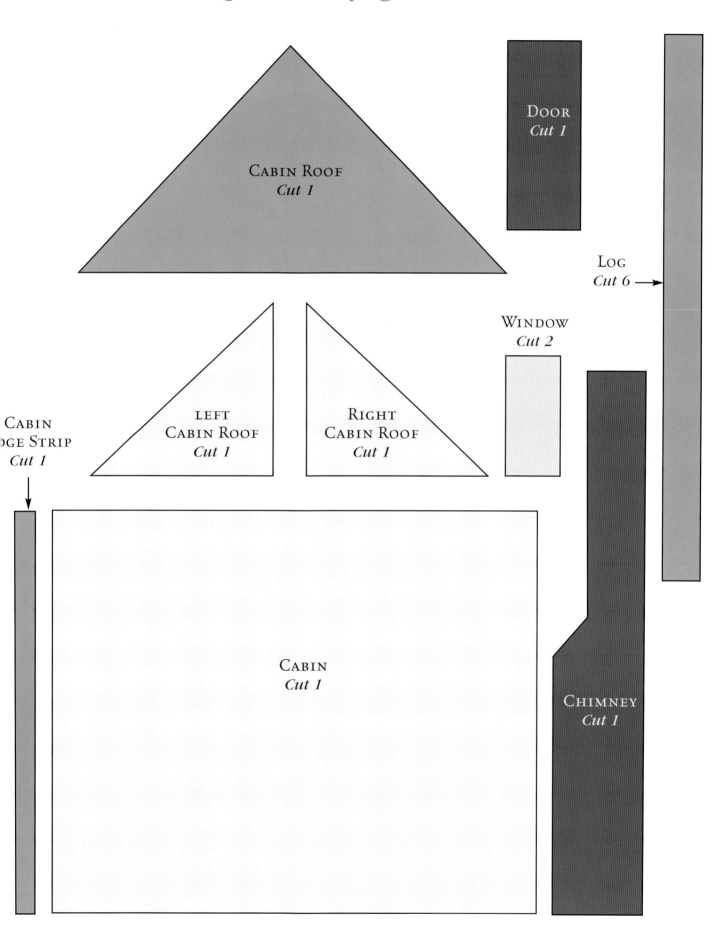

CABIN ROOF
*Cut 1*

DOOR
*Cut 1*

LOG
*Cut 6* →

LEFT
CABIN ROOF
*Cut 1*

RIGHT
CABIN ROOF
*Cut 1*

WINDOW
*Cut 2*

CABIN
ĐGE STRIP
*Cut 1*
↓

CABIN
*Cut 1*

CHIMNEY
*Cut 1*

## Flying Geese Wallhanging

### Materials

*Finished size is approximately 33" x 33"*

Refer to the general instructions on pages 6-7 before starting this project.

*Fabrics are based on 42"-wide cotton fabric that has not been washed.*

One completed Flying Geese block

Scraps of dark green fabric for cornerstones

1/4 yard of cream fabric for sashing

1 yard of medium brown fabric for borders and binding

43" x 43" piece of batting

43" x 43" piece of fabric for backing

### Cutting Instructions

- From the dark green fabric, cut:
  1 strip 2-1/2" x 42"; from this strip, cut:
    4 squares 2-1/2" x 2-1/2"

- From the cream fabric cut:
  2 strips 2-1/2" x 42"; from these strips, cut:
    4 rectangles 2-1/2" x 21-1/2"

- From the medium brown fabric, cut:
  4 strips 4-1/2" x 42"
  5 strips 2-1/2" x 42"

## Assembling the Wallhanging

1. Sew a cream 2-1/2" x 21-1/2" rectangle on each side of the Flying Geese block. Press toward the block.

2. Sew a dark green 2-1/2" x 2-1/2" square on each of 2 cream 2-1/2" x 21-1/2" rectangles. Press toward the dark.

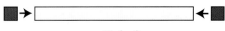

*Make 2*

3. Sew the rectangles from Step 2 to the top and bottom of the Flying Geese block. Press in the direction of least amount of bulk.

4. Measure the width of the wallhanging through the center for the top and bottom border measurement. Cut 2 strips that length from the medium brown 4-1/2"-wide strips. Sew to the top and bottom. Press toward the border.

5. Measure the wallhanging through the center lengthwise for side border measurement. Cut two medium brown strips that length from the 4-1/2"-wide strips. Sew these strips to each side. Press toward the border.

## Finishing the Wallhanging

1. Layer the backing fabric, batting, and wallhanging top.

2. Hand or machine quilt as desired.

3. Finish the wallhanging by sewing on the binding.

# FLYING GEESE SNUGGLER

## Materials

*Finished size is approximately 62" x 74"*

Refer to the general instructions on pages 6-7 before starting this project.

*Fabrics are based on 42"-wide fabric that has not been washed.*

1-3/4 yards of cream fabric for blocks

◼

1-1/8 yards of pale green fabric for blocks and inner border

◼

5/8 yard of light green fabric for blocks

◼

1-1/8 yards of medium green fabric for blocks and middle border

◼

2-1/2 yards of dark green fabric for blocks, outer border and binding

◼

1 yard of very dark green for sashing

◼

70" x 82" piece of batting

◼

5-1/4 yards of fabric for backing

## Flying Geese Blocks

### Cutting Instructions

*(A 1/4" seam allowance is included in these measurements.)*

• From the cream fabric, cut:
  16 strips 3-1/2" x 42"; from these strips, cut:
  192 squares 3-1/2" x 3-1/2"

• From the pale green fabric, cut:
  4 strips 3-1/2" x 42", from these strips, cut:
  24 rectangles 3-1/2" x 6-1/2"
  7 strips 2-1/2" x 42" for inner border

• From the light green fabric, cut:
  4 strips 3-1/2" x 42"; from these strips, cut:
  24 rectangles 3-1/2" x 6-1/2"

• From the medium green fabric, cut:
  4 strips 3-1/2" x 42"; from these strips, cut:
  24 rectangles 3-1/2" x 6-1/2"
  7 strips 2-1/2" x 42" for middle border

• From the dark green fabric, cut:
  4 strips 3-1/2" x 42"; from these strips, cut:
  24 rectangles 3-1/2" x 6-1/2"
  7 strips 5-1/2" x 42" for outer border
  7 strips 3" x 42" for binding

• From the very dark green fabric, cut:
  12 strips 2-1/2" x 42"; from 3 of these strips, cut:
    3 strips into 8 rectangles 2-1/2" x 12-1/2"
  Set aside remaining strips for sashing.

### Assembling the Blocks

1. On the wrong side of the 192 cream 3-1/2" x 3-1/2" squares, draw a diagonal line.

2. Place a 3-1/2" cream square on the right side of the 24 pale green 3-1/2" x 6-1/2" rectangles. Sew on the marked diagonal line. Trim seam allowance to 1/4" and press to make 1 Unit A. You will need 24 Unit A.

*Unit A; Make 24*

3. Place a 3-1/2" cream square on the left side of Unit A. Sew on the marked diagonal line. Trim seam allowance to 1/4" and press to make 1 Unit B. You will need 24 Unit B.

*Unit B; Make 24*

4. Repeat steps 2 and 3 using the 24 light green rectangles, 24 medium green rectangles, and the 24 dark green rectangles.

*Unit C*
*Light Green*
*Make 24*

*Unit D*
*Medium Green*
*Make 24*

*Unit E*
*Dark Green*
*Make 24*

5. Sew 2 Unit B together to make 1 Unit F. Press in the direction of least amount of bulk. You will need 12 Unit F.

*Unit F; Make 12*

6. Repeat step 5 with the light green Unit C, the medium green Unit D, and the dark green Unit E.

*Unit G*
*Light Green*
*Make 12*

*Unit H*
*Medium Green*
*Make 12*

*Unit I*
*Dark Green*
*Make 12*

7. Sew medium green Unit H and pale green Unit F together to make 1 Unit J. Press in the direction of least amount of bulk. You need 12 Unit J.

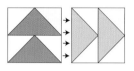 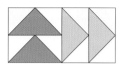

*Unit J; Make 12*

8. Sew light green Unit G and dark green Unit I together as shown to make 1 Unit K. Press in the direction of least amount of bulk. You will need 12 Unit K.

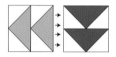 

*Unit K; Make 12*

9. Sew Unit J and Unit K together as shown to make 1 Unit L. Press in the direction of least amount of bulk. You will need 12 Unit L.

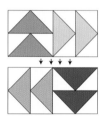 

*Unit L; Make 12*

## Adding the Sashing

1. Sew 2 very dark green 2-1/2" x 12-1/2" rectangles and 3 Unit L together. Press in the direction of least amount of bulk. You will have 4 rows total.

2. Measure a row through the center for sashing strip measurement. Cut 5 very dark green 2-1/2" strips to that length.

3. Sew the strips and rows together. Press in the direction of least amount of bulk.

4. Measure the length of the quilt top through the center for the side sashing measurement. Cut 2 very dark green 2-1/2" strips that length. Sew a strip to each side. Press toward the sashing.

## Adding the Borders

1. Measure the width of the quilt top through the center for the inner border measurement. Cut 2 pale green 2-1/2" strips to that length. Sew the strips to the top and bottom of quilt top. Press toward the border.

2. Measure the length of the quilt top through the center for inner border measurement. Cut 2 pale green 2-1/2" strips to that length. Sew to each side of quilt top. Press toward the border.

3. Repeat steps 1 and 2 for the medium green middle border and the dark green outer border.

## Finishing the Quilt

1. Layer the backing fabric, batting, and the quilt top.

2. Baste the layers together. Hand or machine quilt as desired.

3. Finish the quilt by sewing on the binding.

**Flying Geese Snuggler**

# BEAR PAW BLOCK

*Make the Bear Paw block your catch of the day featured
on a 24-block snuggler with appliqué patterns for a bear bath set
complete with bear tracks stenciled on a cotton rug.*

## Materials

*Finished size is approximately 21" x 21"*

Refer to the general instructions on pages 6-7 before starting this project.

*Fabrics are based on 42"-wide cotton fabric that has not been washed.*

3/4 yard of tan fabric for block

1/2 yard of dark blue fabric for block

1/2 yard of golden brown fabric for block

Scraps of dark black-and-brown fabric for bear body

Scraps of light brown fabric for bear head, inside of the paw prints, and stones

Scraps of tan fabric for muzzle

Scraps of black fabric for paw prints, claws, and nose

Scraps of blue fabric for water

Scraps of medium green fabric for 2 tree tops and fish

Scraps of dark green fabric for tree top

Scraps of medium brown fabric for tree trunks and stones

Scraps of off-white fabric for aspen tree trunk and stones

3/4 yard of fusible web

Stabilizer for appliqués

Sulky® threads to match appliqué fabrics

# Bear Paw Block

## Cutting Instructions

*(A 1/4" seam allowance is included in these measurements.)*

• From the tan fabric, cut:
  1 strip 4-1/4" x 42"; from this strip, cut:
    1 square 4-1/4" x 4-1/4"
  1 strip 4-5/8" x 42"; from this strip, cut:
    3 squares 4-5/8" x 4-5/8", cut squares in half diagonally once to make 6 half-square triangles
  1 strip 11-1/2" x 42"; from this strip, cut:
    2 squares 11-1/2" x 11-1/2", cut squares in half diagonally once to make 4 half-square triangles

• From the dark blue fabric, cut:
  1 strip 4-5/8" x 42"; from this strip, cut:
    3 squares 4-5/8" x 4-5/8"; cut squares in half diagonally once to make 6 half-square triangles
  1 strip 12-1/8" x 42"; from this strip, cut:
    1 square 12-1/8" x 12-1/8"; cut square in half diagonally once to make 2 half-square triangles
  *(Note: 1 half-square triangle will not be used)*

• From the golden brown fabric, cut:
  1 strip 12-1/8" x 42"; from this strip, cut:
    1 square 12-1/8" x 12-1/8"; cut square in half diagonally once to make 2 half-square triangles
  *(Note: 1 half-square triangle will not be used)*

## Assembling the Block

1. Sew the dark blue 4-5/8" half-square triangles and the tan 4-5/8" half-square triangles together to make 1 Unit A. Press toward the dark blue. You will need 6 Unit A.

*Unit A; Make 6*

2. Sew 3 Unit A together, as shown to make 1 Unit B. Press toward the dark blue.

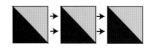 

*Unit B; Make 1*

3. Sew 3 Unit A together, as shown to make 1 Unit C. Press toward the dark blue.

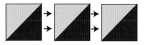

*Unit C; Make 1*

4. Sew the tan 4-1/4" square to Unit B on the left side to make 1 Unit D. Press toward the square.

*Unit D; Make 1*

5. Sew a golden brown 12-1/8" half-square triangle and a dark blue 12-1/8" half-square triangle together to make 1 Unit E. Press toward the dark blue.

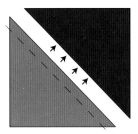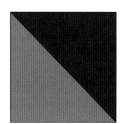

*Unit E; Make 1*

6. Sew Unit C to the left side of Unit E to make 1 Unit F. Press toward the square.

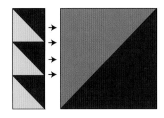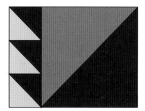

*Unit F; Make 1*

7. Sew Unit D to the top of Unit F to make 1 Unit G. Press toward the square.

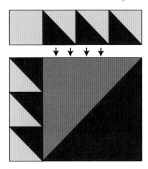

*Unit G; Make 1*

8. Sew 2 tan 11-1/2" half-square triangles to opposite sides of Unit G. Press toward the triangle.

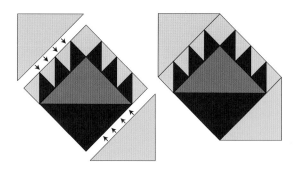

9. Sew the 2 remaining tan 11-1/2" half-square triangles to the remaining sides of Unit G. Press toward the tan triangle.

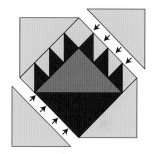

10. Square up the block, if necessary. Leave a 1/4" seam allowance past the intersection and make sure that the corners are at 90-degree angles.

## Adding the Appliqués

1. Trace all appliqué templates from pages 137-139 and cut out.

2. Refer to general instructions to prepare pieces for appliqué.

3. Use lightweight tear-away stabilizer to machine appliqué the pieces. Place the stabilizer beneath the fabric layers and use a small zigzag stitch to sew around each shape, smoothly covering the raw fabric edge. If your machine has stitch options, use them to detail the appliqués. After the stitching is complete, remove the stabilizer according to the manufacturer's instructions.

# Templates for Bear Paw Block

**STONE A1**
*Cut 1*

**STONE A2**
*Cut 1*

**STONE A3**
*Cut 1*

**STONE B**
*Cut 1*

**STONE C**
*Cut 1*

**STONE D1**
*Cut 1*

**STONE D2**
*Cut 1*

**STONE E1**
*Cut 1*

**STONE E2**
*Cut 1*

**TREE TOP**
*Cut 3*

**TREE TOP**
*Cut 3*

**TREE TRUNK**
*Cut 3*

# Templates for Bear Paw Block

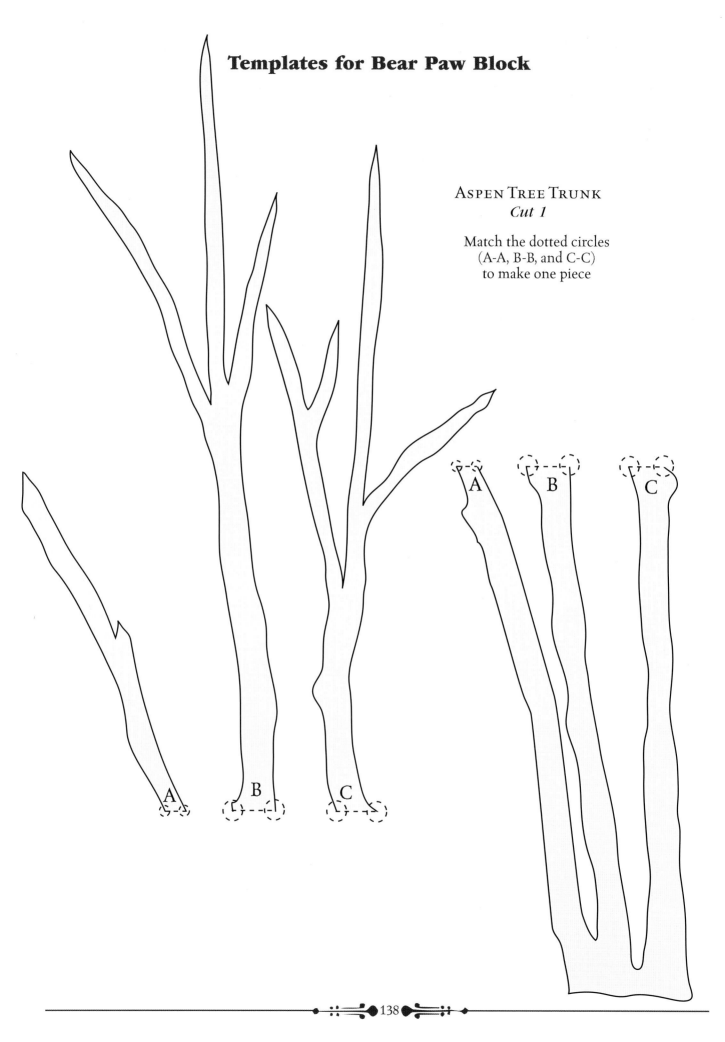

ASPEN TREE TRUNK
*Cut 1*

Match the dotted circles
(A-A, B-B, and C-C)
to make one piece

A

B

C

A

B

C

# Templates for Bear Paw Block

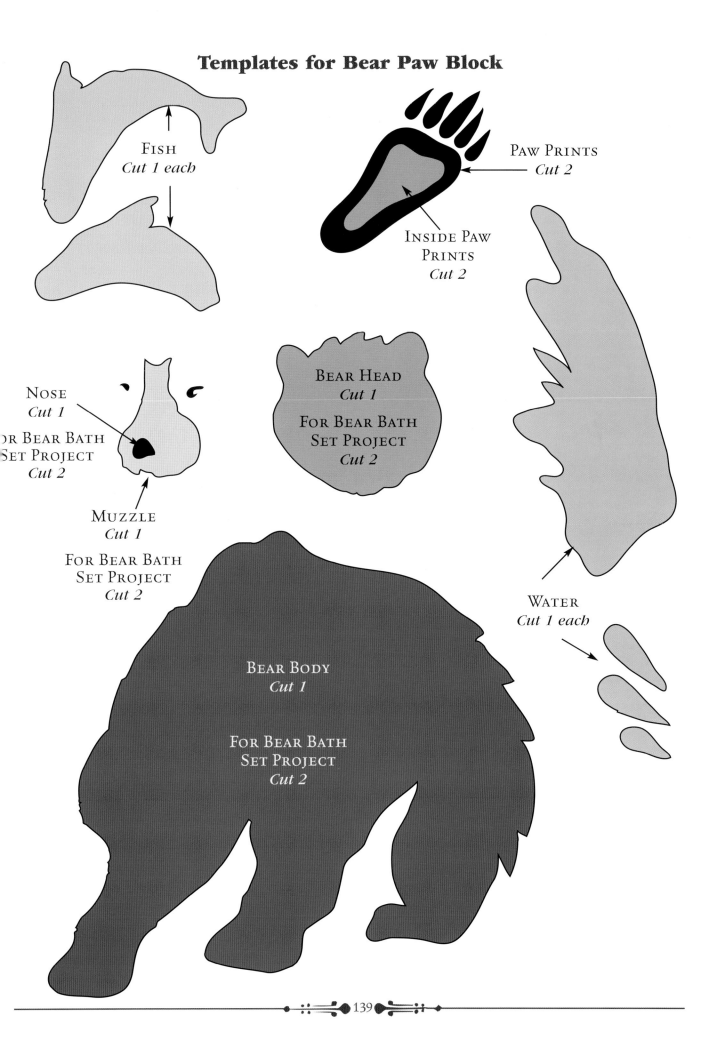

**FISH**
*Cut 1 each*

**PAW PRINTS**
*Cut 2*

**INSIDE PAW PRINTS**
*Cut 2*

**NOSE**
*Cut 1*

**FOR BEAR BATH SET PROJECT**
*Cut 2*

**MUZZLE**
*Cut 1*

**FOR BEAR BATH SET PROJECT**
*Cut 2*

**BEAR HEAD**
*Cut 1*

**FOR BEAR BATH SET PROJECT**
*Cut 2*

**WATER**
*Cut 1 each*

**BEAR BODY**
*Cut 1*

**FOR BEAR BATH SET PROJECT**
*Cut 2*

# Bear Paw Snuggler

## Materials

*Finished size is approximately 61" x 85"*

Refer to the general instructions on pages 6-7 before starting this project.

*Fabrics are based on 42"-wide cotton fabric that has not been washed.*

3-3/4 yards of dark blue fabric for blocks, outer border, and binding
▪
1 yard of golden brown fabric for blocks
▪
1-5/8 yards of cream fabric for sashing
▪
1/4 yard of black fabric for cornerstones
▪
69" x 93" piece of batting
▪
5-1/2 yards of fabric for backing

## Bear Paw Blocks

Make 24

*Cutting Instructions*

*(A 1/4" seam allowance is included in these measurements.)*

- From the dark blue fabric, cut:

  4 strips 6-1/2" x 42"; from these strips, cut:

  24 squares 6-1/2" x 6-1/2"

  5 strips 3-7/8" x 42"; from these strips, cut:

  48 squares 3-7/8" x 3-7/8"; cut squares in half diagonally to make 96 half-square triangles

  1 strip 3-1/2" x 42"; from this strip, cut:

  6 squares 3-1/2" x 3-1/2"

  8 strips 5-1/2" x 42" for the outer border

  7 strips 3" x 42" for binding

- From the golden brown fabric, cut:

  2 strips 3-1/2" x 42"; from these strips, cut:

  24 squares 3-1/2" x 3-1/2"

  5 strips 3-7/8" x 42"; from this strip, cut:

  48 squares 3-7/8" x 3-7/8"; cut squares in half diagonally to make 96 half-square triangles

- From the cream fabric, cut:

  6 strips 3-1/2" x 42"; from these strips, cut:

  24 rectangles 3-1/2" x 9-1/2"

  9 strips 3-1/2" x 42"; from this strip, cut:

  17 rectangles 3-1/2" x 21-1/2"

- From the black fabric, cut:

  1 strip 3-1/2" x 42"; from these strips, cut:

  12 squares 3-1/2" x 3-1/2"

## Assembling the Block

1. Sew a dark blue 3-7/8" triangle and a golden brown 3-7/8" triangle together to make 1 Unit A. Press toward the dark. You will need 96 Unit A.

*Unit A; Make 96*

2. Sew 2 Unit A together, as shown to make 1 Unit B. Press toward the dark. You will need 24 Unit B.

*Unit B; Make 24*

3. Sew 2 Unit A together, as shown to make 1 Unit C. Press toward the dark blue. You will need 24 Unit C.

*Unit C; Make 24*

4. Sew a golden brown 3-1/2" square to the left side of a Unit B to make 1 Unit D. Press toward the square. You will need 24 Unit D.

*Unit D; Make 24*

5. Sew a Unit C to the left side of a dark blue 6-1/2" square to make 1 Unit E. Press toward the square. You will need 24 Unit E.

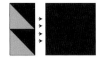

*Unit E; Make 24*

6. Sew a Unit D to the top of Unit E, as shown to make 1 Unit F. Press toward the square. You will need 24 Unit F.

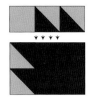

*Unit F; Make 24*

# Adding the Sashing

1. Sew a dark blue 3-1/2" square and 2 cream 3-1/2" x 9-1/2" rectangles together to make 1 Unit G. Press toward the cream rectangles. You will need 6 Unit G.

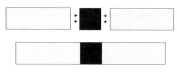

*Unit G; Make 6*

2. Sew a cream 3-1/2" x 9-1/2" rectangle and 2 Unit F together to make 1 Unit H. Press towards the cream rectangle. You will need 12 Unit H.

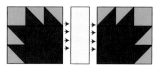

*Unit H; Make 12*

3. Sew a Unit G and 2 Unit H together to make 1 Unit I. Press in the direction of the least amount of bulk. You will need 6 Unit I.

*Unit I; Make 6*

4. Sew 2 cream 3-1/2" x 21-1/2" rectangles, and 2 Unit I together to make 1 Unit J. Press towards the cream rectangles. You will need 3 Unit J.

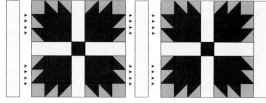

*Unit J; Make 3*

5. Sew 2 cream 3-1/2" x 21-1/2" rectangles and 3 black 3-1/2" squares together to make 1 Unit K. Press toward the cream. You will need 4 Unit K.

*Unit K; Make 4*

6. Sew a Unit K to the top of each Unit J. Sew the remaining Unit K to the bottom of Unit J.

## Adding the Borders

1. Measure the width of the quilt top through the center to get the top and bottom border measurement. Cut 2 strips to that length from the dark blue 5-1/2" strips. Sew to the top and bottom of the quilt. Press toward the border.

2. Measure the length of the quilt top through the top to get the side border measurement. Cut 2 strips to that length from the dark blue 5-1/2" strips. Sew a strip to each side of the quilt top. Press toward the border.

## Finishing the Quilt

1. Layer the quilt backing fabric, batting, and quilt top. Baste the layers together.

2. Hand or machine quilt as desired.

3. Finish the quilt by sewing on the binding.

**Bear Paw Snuggler**

# Bear Bath Set

## *Materials*

Refer to the general instructions on pages 6-7 before starting this project.

### *Bath and Hand Towel*

Purchased bath and hand towel

∎

1/4 yard of black fabric for
bears' bodies, tip of nose and paw prints

∎

6" x 6" piece of brown fabric for bears' heads

∎

4" x 4" piece of tan fabric for bears' muzzles

∎

8" x 8" piece of green fabric for trees

∎

Stabilizer

∎

3/4 yard of fusible web

∎

Sulky® threads to match appliqués

### *Stenciled Rug*

Purchased cotton rug

∎

Black permanent marker

∎

Black acrylic paint

∎

Stencil brush

∎

1 sheet of template plastic

∎

Art knife

## Adding the Appliqués

1. Trace all appliqué templates from page 139 and 145 and cut out.

2. Refer to general instructions to prepare pieces for appliqué.

3. Use lightweight tear-away stabilizer to machine appliqué the pieces. Place the stabilizer beneath the fabric layers and use a small zigzag stitch to sew around each shape, smoothly covering the raw fabric edge. If your machine has stitch options, use them to detail the appliqués. After the stitching is complete, remove the stabilizer according to the manufacturer's instructions.

## Stenciled Bear Tracks Rug

1. With a black permanent marker, trace one pair of bear paw prints onto template plastic. Paws can be arranged unevenly to resemble a bear walking.

2. Cut out within the traced lines with the art knife. Try to cut as smoothly as possible to avoid jagged edges.

3. Place a piece of cardboard under rug before starting. Pour a small amount of black paint into a tray. Dip stencil brush into the paint. Dab once on a piece of paper towel to eliminate excess paint. Stencil with a dabbing motion inside cut-out parts of template.

4. When complete, carefully lift template off the rug and wait for the paint to dry thoroughly.

5. Move template forward and stencil another pair of tracks.

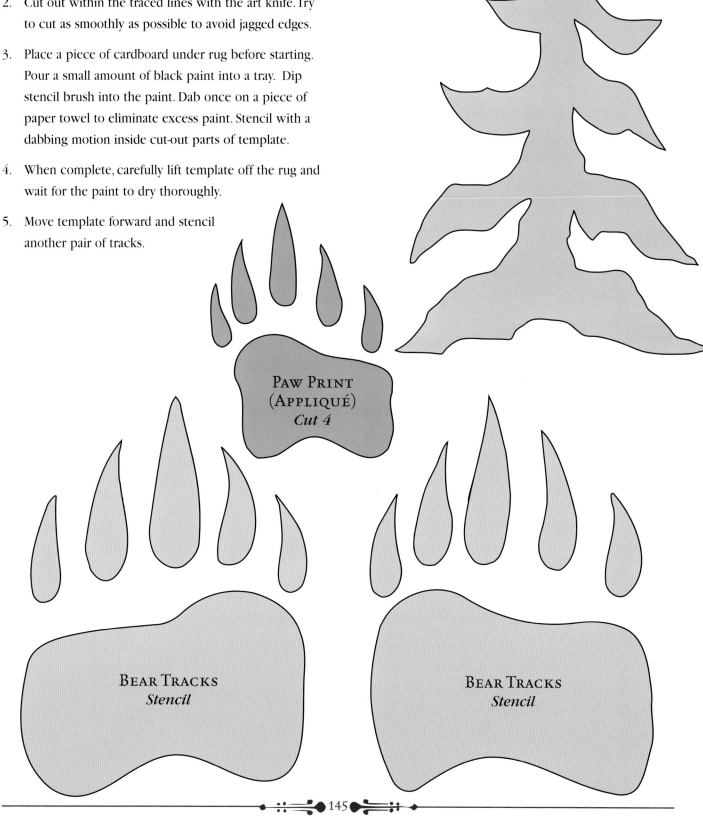

TREE
*Cut 2*

PAW PRINT
(APPLIQUÉ)
*Cut 4*

BEAR TRACKS
*Stencil*

BEAR TRACKS
*Stencil*

# LOG CABIN BLOCK

The Log Cabin block set on point is an easy way to build a
stunning 6-block snuggler and the perfect background to appliqué
a lonely loon and lilies on a waterfowl wallhanging and bath set.

## Materials

*Finished size is approximately 21" x 21"*

Refer to the general instructions on pages 6-7 before starting this project.

*Fabrics are based on 42" wide cotton fabric that has not been washed.*

1/4 yard of cream fabric for background

5/8 yard sky blue fabric for background

1/6 yard of dark blue fabric for background

1/6 yard of royal blue fabric for background

1/6 yard of medium blue fabric for background

1/4 yard total of 3 assorted green fabrics for lily pads and lily stem

Scraps of off-white fabric for clouds

Scraps of black fabric for loon wings and head

Scraps of white fabric for loon neck and lily buds

Scraps of pale yellow fabric for lilies

Scraps of gold fabric for lily centers

Scraps of medium blue for water

1 yard of fusible web

Stabilizer for appliqués

Sulky® threads to match appliqué fabrics

# Log Cabin Block

## Cutting Instructions

*(A 1/4" seam allowance is included in these measurements.)*

• From the cream fabric, cut:
  2 strips 2-5/8" x 42"; from these strips, cut:
      1 rectangle 2-5/8" x 4-3/4"
      1 rectangle 2-5/8" x 6-7/8"
      1 rectangle 2-5/8" x 9"
      1 rectangle 2-5/8" x 11-1/8"
      1 rectangle 2-5/8" x 13-1/4"
      1 rectangle 2-5/8" x 15-3/8"

• From the sky blue fabric, cut:
  1 strip 2-5/8" x 42"; from this strip, cut:
      1 rectangle 2-5/8" x 4-3/4"
  1 strip 11-1/2" x 42"; from this strip, cut:
      2 squares 11-1/2" x 11-1/2" ; cut squares in half diagonally to make 4 half-square triangles

• From the royal blue fabric, cut:
  1 strip 2-5/8" x 42"; from this strip, cut:
      1 square 2-5/8" x 2-5/8"
      1 rectangle 2-5/8" x 11-1/8"
      1 rectangle 2-5/8" x 13-1/4"

• From the medium blue fabric, cut:
  1 strip 2-5/8" x 42"; from this strip, cut:
      1 rectangle 2-5/8" x 6-7/8"

• From the dark blue fabric, cut:
  1 strip 2-5/8" x 42"; from this strip, cut:
      1 square 2-5/8" x 2-5/8"
      1 rectangle 2-5/8" x 9"

## Assembling the Block

1. Sew a dark blue 2-5/8" square and a royal blue 2-5/8" square together to make 1 Unit A. Press toward the dark blue. Square up the block, if necessary.

*Unit A; Make 1*

2. Sew a sky blue 2-5/8" x 4-3/4" rectangle to Unit A, as shown to make 1 Unit B. Press toward the light blue. Square up the block, if necessary.

*Unit B ; Make 1*

3. Sew a cream 2-5/8" x 4-3/4" rectangle to Unit B to make 1 Unit C. Press toward the cream. Square up the block, if necessary.

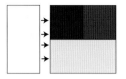

*Unit C; Make 1*

4. Sew a cream 2-5/8" x 6-7/8" rectangle to Unit C to make 1 Unit D. Press toward the cream. Square up the block, if necessary.

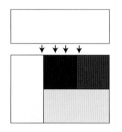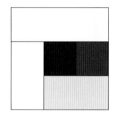

*Unit D; Make 1*

5. Sew a medium blue 2-5/8" x 6-7/8" rectangle to Unit D to make 1 Unit E. Press toward the medium blue. Square up the block, if necessary.

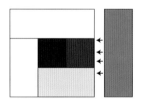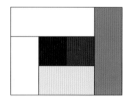

*Unit E; Make 1*

6. Sew a dark blue 2-5/8" x 9" rectangle to Unit E to make 1 Unit F. Press toward the dark blue. Square up the block, if necessary.

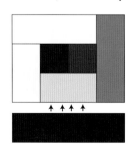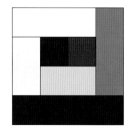

*Unit F; Make 1*

7. Sew a cream 2-5/8" x 9" rectangle to Unit F to make 1 Unit G. Press toward the cream. Square up the block, if necessary.

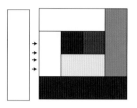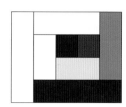

*Unit G; Make 1*

8. Sew a cream 2-5/8" x 11-1/8" rectangle to Unit G to make 1 Unit H. Press toward the cream. Square up the block, if necessary.

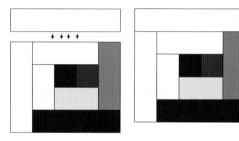

*Unit H; Make 1*

9. Sew a royal blue 2-5/8" x 11-1/8" rectangle to Unit H to make 1 Unit I. Press toward the royal blue. Square up the block, if necessary.

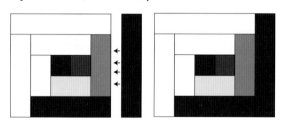

*Unit I; Make 1*

10. Sew a royal blue 2-5/8" x 13-1/4" rectangle to Unit I to make 1 Unit J. Press toward the royal blue. Square up the block, if necessary.

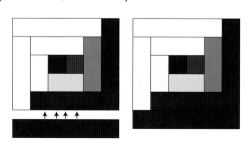

*Unit J; Make 1*

11. Sew a cream 2-5/8" x 13-1/4" rectangle to Unit J to make 1 Unit K. Press toward the cream. Square up the block, if necessary.

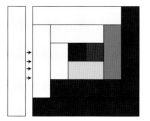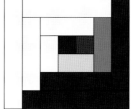

*Unit K; Make 1*

12. Sew a cream 2-5/8" x 15-3/8" rectangle to Unit K to make 1 Unit L. Press toward the cream. Square up the block, if necessary.

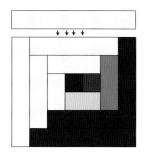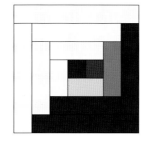

*Unit L; Make 1*

13. Sew 2 sky blue 11-1/2" half-square triangles to opposite sides of the block, as shown. Press carefully toward the triangles.

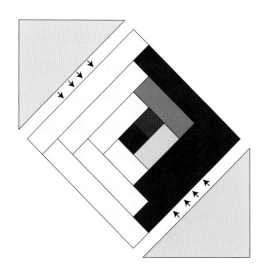

14. Sew 2 sky blue 11-1/2" half-square triangles to the remaining two sides of the block, as shown. Press carefully toward the triangle. Square up the block, if necessary. Make sure to leave a 1/4" seam allowance past the intersections and make sure that the corners are at 90-degree angles.

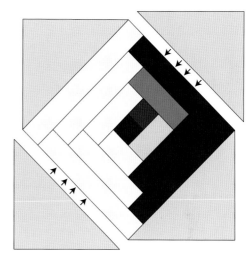

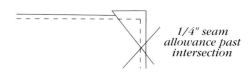

*1/4" seam allowance past intersection*

## Adding the Appliqués

1. Trace all appliqué templates from pages 150-151 and cut out.

2. Refer to general instructions to prepare pieces for appliqué.

3. Use lightweight tear-away stabilizer to machine appliqué the pieces. Place the stabilizer beneath the fabric layers and use a small zigzag stitch to sew around each shape, smoothly covering the raw fabric edge. If your machine has stitch options, use them to detail the appliqués. After the stitching is complete, remove the stabilizer according to the manufacturer's instructions.

# Templates for Log Cabin Block

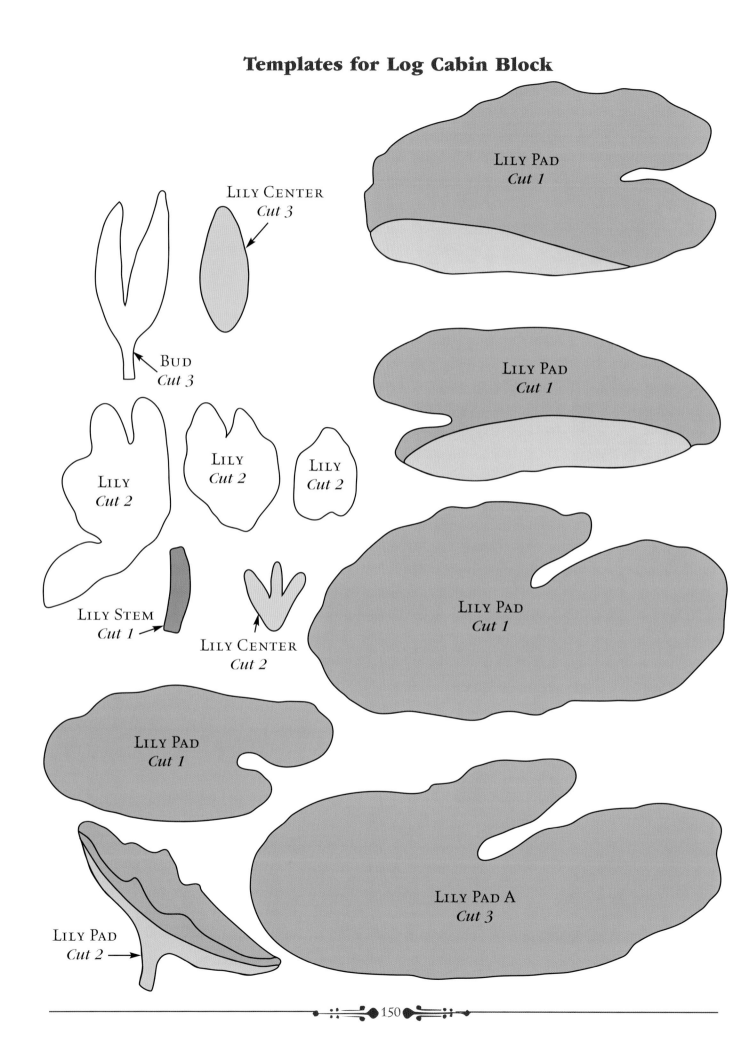

LILY PAD
*Cut 1*

LILY CENTER
*Cut 3*

BUD
*Cut 3*

LILY
*Cut 2*

LILY
*Cut 2*

LILY
*Cut 2*

LILY PAD
*Cut 1*

LILY STEM
*Cut 1*

LILY CENTER
*Cut 2*

LILY PAD
*Cut 1*

LILY PAD
*Cut 1*

LILY PAD A
*Cut 3*

LILY PAD
*Cut 2*

# Templates for Log Cabin Block

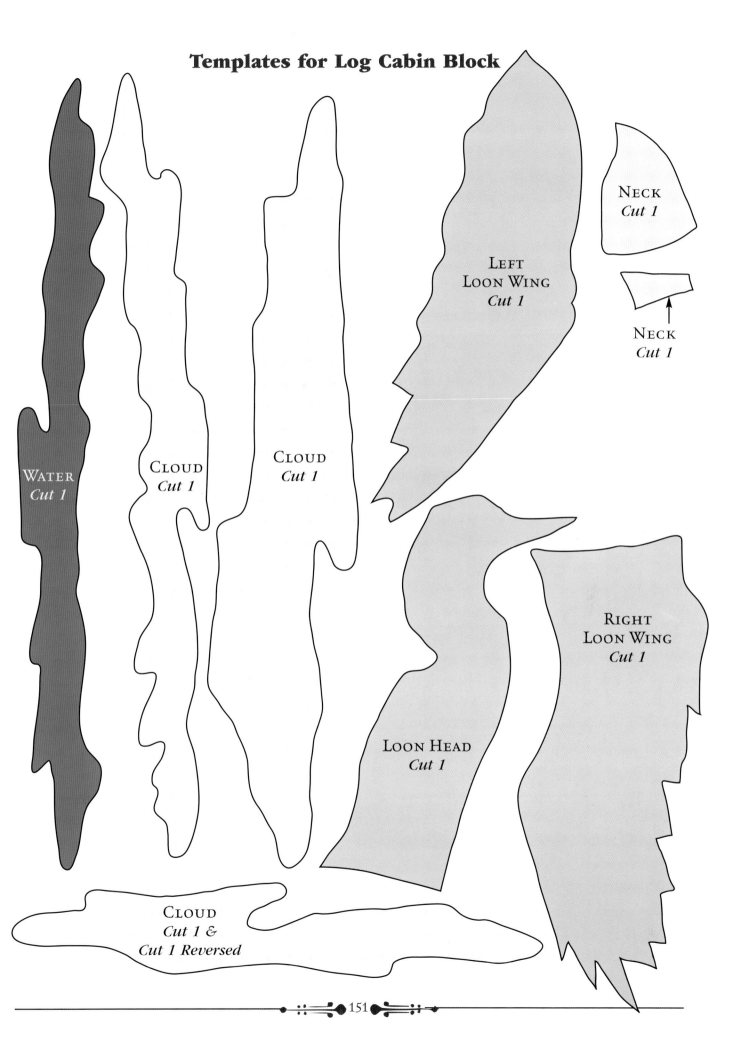

NECK
*Cut 1*

LEFT
LOON WING
*Cut 1*

NECK
*Cut 1*

WATER
*Cut 1*

CLOUD
*Cut 1*

CLOUD
*Cut 1*

RIGHT
LOON WING
*Cut 1*

LOON HEAD
*Cut 1*

CLOUD
*Cut 1 &*
*Cut 1 Reversed*

# Quilt it Quick

# Log Cabin Wallhanging

## Materials

*Finished size is approximately 33" x 33"*

*Refer to the general instructions on pages 6-7 before starting this project.*

*Fabrics are based on 42"-wide cotton fabric that has not been washed.*

One completed Log Cabin Block

∎

Scraps of medium blue fabric for cornerstones

∎

1/3 yard of cream fabric for sashing

∎

1 yard of royal blue fabric for borders and binding

∎

43" x 43" piece of batting

∎

## Cutting Instructions

• From the medium blue fabric, cut:
    4 squares 2-1/2" x 2-1/2" for cornerstones

• From the cream fabric, cut:
    4 strips 2-1/2" x 42"; from these strips, cut:
        4 rectangles 2-1/2" x 21-1/2"

• From the royal blue fabric, cut:
    4 strips 4-1/2" x 42"
    5 strips 2-1/2" x 42"

## Assembling the Wallhanging

1. Sew a cream 2-1/2" x 21-1/2" rectangle on each side of the Log Cabin block. Press toward the block.

2. Sew a medium blue 2-1/2" x 2-1/2" square on each of 2 cream 2-1/2" x 21-1/2" rectangles. Press toward the blue.

*Make 2*

3. Sew rectangles from Step 2 to the top and bottom of the Log Cabin block. Press in the direction of least amount of bulk.

4. Measure the width of the wallhanging through the center to get top and bottom border measurement. Cut two strips to that length from the royal blue 4-1/2" wide strips. Sew strips to the top and bottom. Press toward the border.

5. Measure the length of the wallhanging through the center for side border measurement. Cut two royal blue strips to that length from the 4-1/2"-wide strips. Sew to each side. Press toward the border.

## Finishing the Wallhanging

1. Layer the backing fabric, batting, and wallhanging top.

2. Hand or machine quilt as desired.

3. Finish the wallhanging by sewing on the binding.

# Lonely Loon Bath Set

## Materials

*Refer to the general instructions on pages 6-7 before starting this project.*

Purchased bath, hand towel, and washcloth set

■

9" x 9" piece of black fabric for
loon wings and head

■

5" x 5" piece of white fabric
for lily buds and loon neck

■

4" x 9" piece of medium blue fabric for water

■

4" x 4" piece of pale yellow fabric for lily centers

■

8" x 8" piece of light green fabric for lily pads

■

6" x 6" piece of dark green fabric for lily pads

■

1/2 yard fusible web

■

Stabilizer

■

Sulky® threads to match appliqués

## Adding the Appliqués

1. Trace appliqué templates from pages 150-151 and cut out.

2. Refer to general instructions to prepare pieces for appliqué.

3. Use lightweight tear-away stabilizer to machine appliqué the pieces. Place the stabilizer beneath the fabric layers and use a small zigzag stitch to sew around each shape, smoothly covering the raw fabric edge. If your machine has stitch options, use them to detail the appliqués. After the stitching is complete, remove the stabilizer according to the manufacturer's instructions.

# LOG CABIN SNUGGLER

## Materials

**Finished size is approximately 60" x 81"**

Refer to the general instructions on pages 6-7 before starting this project.

*Fabric is based on 40"-wide flannel fabric that has not been washed.*

7/8 yard of navy blue flannel
for blocks and triangles

■

3/8 yard of bright blue flannel for blocks

■

1/4 yard of light blue flannel for blocks

■

7/8 yard of rust flannel for blocks and triangles

■

1/2 yard of tan flannel for blocks

■

1/3 yard of cocoa flannel for blocks

■

3 yards of gold flannel for blocks, triangles, the outer border, and the binding

■

1/3 yard of medium blue flannel for blocks

■

1/2 yard of green flannel for triangles

■

7/8 yard of dark green flannel for the inner border

■

A 68" x 89" piece of batting

■

5-1/2 yards of flannel for backing

## Log Cabin Blocks

**Make 6 blocks**

### Cutting instructions

*(Measurements include a 1/4" seam allowance)*

• From the navy blue flannel, cut:
  4 strips 2-5/8" x 40"; from these strips, cut:
  6 squares 2-5/8" x 2-5/8"
  6 rectangles 2-5/8" x 6-7/8"
  6 rectangles 2-5/8" x 13-1/4"
  1 strip 11-1/2" x 40"; from this strip, cut:
  3 squares 11-1/2" x 11-1/2"; cut each square diagonally to make 6 half-square triangles

• From the bright blue flannel, cut:
  3 strips 2-5/8" x 40"; from these strips, cut:
  6 squares 2-5/8" x 2-5/8"
  6 rectangles 2-5/8" x 9"

• From the light blue flannel, cut:
  1 strip 2-5/8" x 40"; from this strip, cut:
  6 rectangles 2-5/8" x 4-3/4"

• From the rust flannel, cut:
  4 strips 2-5/8" x 40"; from these strips, cut:
  6 rectangles 2-5/8" x 4-3/4"
  6 rectangles 2-5/8" x 15-3/8"
  1 strip 11-1/2" x 40"; from this strip, cut:
  3 squares 11-1/2" x 11-1/2"; cut each square diagonally to make 6 half-square triangles

• From the tan flannel, cut:
  4 strips 2-5/8" x 40"; from these strips, cut:
  6 rectangles 2-5/8" x 6-7/8"
  6 rectangles 2-5/8" x 13-1/4"

- From the cocoa flannel, cut:

  2 strips 2-5/8" x 40"; from these strips, cut:

  6 rectangles 2-5/8" x 9"

- From the gold flannel, cut:

  2 strips 2-5/8" x 40"; from these strips, cut:

  6 rectangles 2-5/8" x 11-1/8"

  1 strip 11-1/2" x 40"; from this strip, cut:

  3 squares 11-1/2" x 11-1/2", cut each square diagonally to make 6 half-square triangles

  8 strips 6-1/2" x 40" for outer border

  8 strips 3" x 40" for binding

- From the medium blue flannel, cut:

  2 strips 2-5/8" x 40"; from these strips, cut:

  6 rectangles 2-5/8" x 11-1/8"

- From the green flannel, cut:

  1 strip 11-1/2" x 40"; from this strip, cut:

  3 squares 11-1/2" x 11-1/2", cut each square diagonally to make 6 half-square triangles

- From the dark green flannel, cut:

  7 strips 3-1/2" x 40" for the inner border

## Assembling the Log Cabin Blocks

1.  Sew together a navy blue 2-5/8" square and a bright blue 2-5/8" square to make 1 Unit A. Press the seam toward the navy blue, squaring up the block if necessary. You will need 6 Unit A.

*Unit A; Make 6*

2.  Sew a light blue 2-5/8" x 4-3/4" rectangle to Unit A to make 1 Unit B. Press the seam toward the light blue, squaring up the block if necessary. You will need 6 Unit B.

*Unit B; Make 6*

3.  Sew a rust 2-5/8" x 4-3/4" rectangle to Unit B to make 1 Unit C. Press the seam toward the rust, squaring up the block if necessary. You will need 6 Unit C.

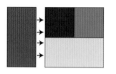

*Unit C; Make 6*

4.  Sew a tan 2-5/8" x 6-7/8" rectangle to Unit C to make 1 Unit D. Press the seam toward the tan, squaring up the block if necessary. You will need 6 Unit D.

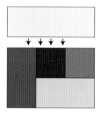

*Unit D; Make 6*

5.  Sew a navy blue 2-5/8" x 6-7/8" rectangle to Unit D to make 1 Unit E. Press the seam toward the navy blue, squaring up the block if necessary. You will need 6 Unit E.

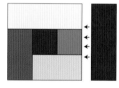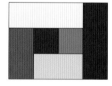

*Unit E; Make 6*

6.  Sew a bright blue 2-5/8" x 9" rectangle to Unit E to make 1 Unit F. Press the seam toward the bright blue, squaring up the block if necessary. You will need 6 Unit F.

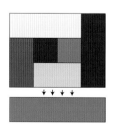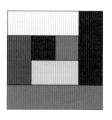

*Unit F; Make 6*

7. Sew a cocoa 2-5/8" x 9" rectangle to Unit F to make 1
Unit G. Press the seam toward the cocoa, squaring up
the block if necessary. You will need 6 Unit G.

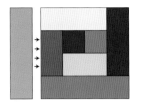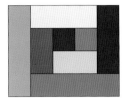

*Unit G; Make 6*

8. Sew a gold 2-5/8" x 11-1/8" rectangle to Unit G to
make 1 Unit H. Press the seam toward the gold, squaring up the block if necessary. You will need 6 Unit H.

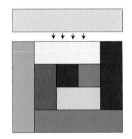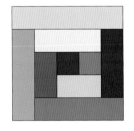

*Unit H; Make 6*

9. Sew a medium blue 2-5/8" x 11-1/8" rectangle to
Unit H to make 1 Unit I. Press the seam toward the
medium blue, squaring up the block if necessary.
You will need 6 Unit I.

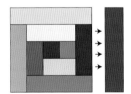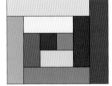

*Unit I; Make 6*

10. Sew a navy blue 2-5/8" x 13-1/4" rectangle to Unit I.
Press the seam toward the navy blue, squaring up the
block if necessary. You will need 6 Unit J.

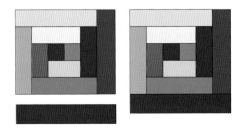

*Unit J; Make 6*

11. Sew a tan 2-5/8" x 13-1/4" rectangle to Unit J to make
1 Unit K. Press the seam toward the tan, squaring up
the block if necessary. You will need 6 Unit K.

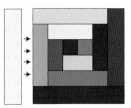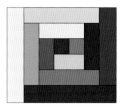

*Unit K; Make 6*

12. Sew a rust 2-5/8" x 15-3/8" rectangle to Unit K to
make 1 Unit L. Press the seam toward the rust,
squaring up the block if necessary. You will need 6
Unit L.

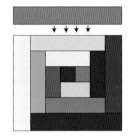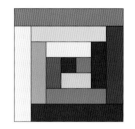

*Unit L; Make 6*

13. On each of the 6 blocks, sew the navy blue 11-1/2"
triangle on the rust side of the block, and then sew
the gold 11-1/2" triangle on the navy blue side of the
block. Carefully press the seams toward the triangles.

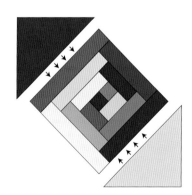

14. On each of the 6 blocks, sew the green 11-1/2" triangle on the medium blue side of the block, and then sew the rust 11-1/2" triangle on the tan side of the block. Carefully press the seams toward the triangles, squaring up the block if necessary.

15. To complete the quilt top, sew the 6 blocks together in three rows of two blocks. Press the seams in the direction of the least bulk.

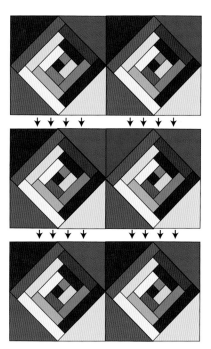

## Adding the Borders

1. Measure the width of the quilt top through the center and cut 2 dark green 3-1/2" strips to that measurement. Sew these strips to the top and bottom edges of the quilt top. Press the seams toward the border.

2. Measure the length of the quilt top through the center and cut 2 dark green 3-1/2" strips to that measurement. Sew these strips to the side edges of the quilt top. Press the seams toward the border.

3. Measure the new width of the quilt top through the center and cut 2 gold 6-1/2" strips to that measurement. Sew these strips to the top and bottom edges of the inner border. Press the seams toward the border.

4. Measure the new length of the quilt top through the center and cut 2 gold 6-1/2" strips to that measurement. Sew these strips to the side edges of the inner border. Press the seams toward the border.

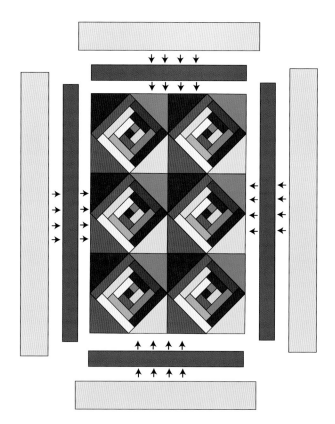

## Finishing the Quilt

1. Layer the quilt backing fabric, the batting, and quilt top. Baste the layers together.

2. Hand or machine stitch the quilt as desired.

3. Finish the quilt by sewing on the binding.

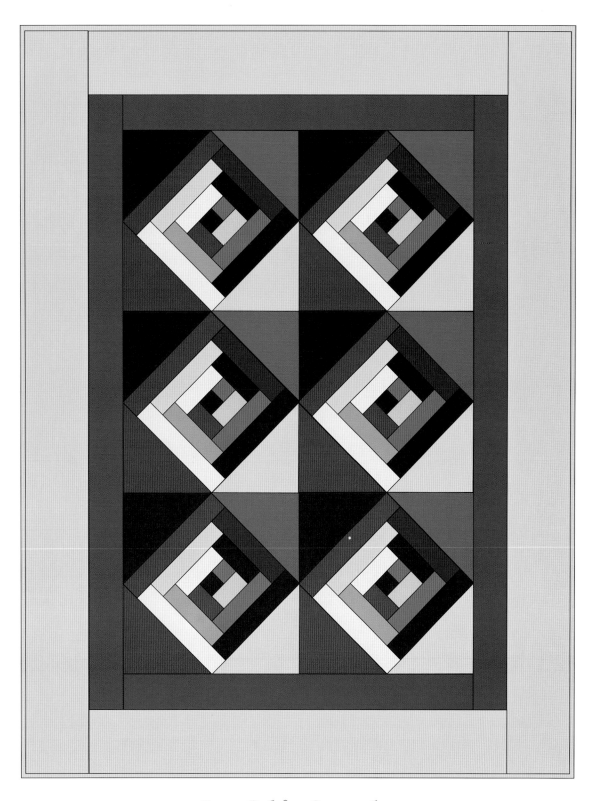

**Log Cabin Snuggler**

Shades of autumn are reminders of fall's first frost. The classic Maple Leaf block serves as the background for a scene featuring a family of deer and a scattering of falling leaves to appliqué on a wildlife wallhanging.

## Materials

*Finished size is approximately 21" x 21"*

Refer to the general instructions on pages 6-7 before starting this project.

*Fabrics are based on 42"-wide cotton fabric that has not been washed.*

7/8 yard of pale yellow fabric for background

1/4 yard of salmon fabric for background

1/4 yard of burnt orange fabric for background

1/4 yard of golden brown fabric for background

1/4 yard of brown fabric for background

1/4 yard of green fabric for background and stem on maple leaf

1/4 yard of dark green fabric for tree tops and maple leaves

Scraps of light and medium green fabric for maple leaves

Scraps of rust fabric for maple leaves

Scraps of light brown fabric for fawn and antlers

Scraps of medium brown fabric for doe

Scraps of dark brown fabric for buck and tree trunks

Scraps of blue fabric for water

1 yard of fusible web

Stabilizer for appliqués

Sulky® threads to match appliqué fabrics

## Maple Leaf Block

### Cutting Instructions

*(A 1/4" seam allowance is included in these measurements.)*

- From the pale yellow fabric, cut:
  1 strip 5-1/2" x 42"; from this strip, cut:
     2 squares 5-1/2" x 5-1/2"
  1 strip 5-7/8" x 42"; from this strip, cut:
     2 squares 5-7/8" x 5-7/8"; cut squares in half diagonally to make 4 half-square triangles
  1 strip 11-1/2" x 42"; from this strip, cut:
     2 squares 11-1/2" x 11-1/2", cut squares in half diagonally to make 4 half-square triangles

- From the salmon fabric, cut:
  1 strip 5-1/2" x 42"; from this strip, cut:
     1 square 5-1/2" x 5-1/2"

- From the burnt orange fabric, cut:
  1 strip 5-1/2" x 42"; from this strip, cut:
     1 square 5-1/2" x 5-1/2"

- From the golden brown fabric, cut:
  1 strip 5-1/2" x 42"; from this strip, cut:
     1 square 5-1/2" x 5-1/2"

- From the brown fabric, cut:
  1 strip 5-7/8" x 42"; from this strip, cut:
     2 squares 5-7/8" x 5-7/8"; cut squares in half diagonally to make 4 half-square triangles

- From the green fabric, cut:
  1 strip 4-1/2" x 42"; from this strip, cut:
     4 squares 4-1/2" x 4-1/2"
  1 rectangle 1-1/4" x 8" for stem on maple leaf

### Assembling the Block

1. Sew a pale yellow 5-7/8" triangle and a brown 5-7/8" triangle together to make 1 Unit A. Press toward the brown. You will need 4 Unit A.

*Unit A; Make 4*

2. Sew 2 Unit A and a 5-1/2" pale yellow square together, as shown. Press in the direction of least amount of bulk. This will be Row 1.

*Row 1*

3. Sew the golden brown and the burnt orange 5-1/2" square and one Unit A together. Press in the direction of least amount of bulk. This will be Row 2.

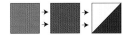

*Row 2*

4. Following manufacturer's instructions, fuse web to the wrong side of the green 1-1/4" x 8" rectangle. Trim rectangle to 3/4" wide. Fuse the stem on the diagonal center of the 5-1/2" pale yellow square. Machine stitch using a small zigzag down each long edge of the stem. Trim stem off at each corner.

5. Sew the appliquéd pale yellow 5-1/2" square, the salmon 5-1/2" square and one Unit A together, as shown. Press in the direction of least amount of bulk. This will be Row 3.

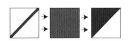

*Row 3*

6. Sew Row 1, Row 2, and Row 3 together, as shown. Press in the direction of least amount of bulk.

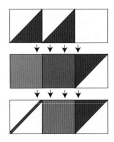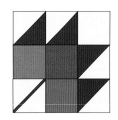

Row 1
Row 2
Row 3

7. Sew two pale yellow 11-1/2" triangles on opposite sides of the block. Press carefully toward the triangle.

8. Sew the two remaining pale yellow 11-1/2" triangles on the remaining sides of the block, as shown. Press carefully toward the triangles. Square up the block, if necessary. Make sure to leave a 1/4" seam allowance past the intersections and make sure the corners are at 90-degree angles.

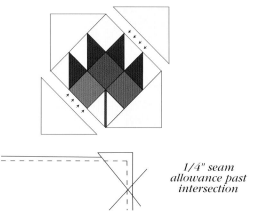

*1/4" seam allowance past intersection*

9. Draw a diagonal line on the wrong side of the green 4-1/2" squares, as shown.

10. Sew the 4-1/2" green squares on each pale yellow triangle on the marked diagonal line, as shown. Press the green triangle toward the outside. Trim away the middle triangle only.

## Adding the Appliqués

1. Trace all appliqué templates from pages 165-167 and cut out.

2. Refer to general instructions to prepare pieces for appliqué.

3. Use lightweight tear-away stabilizer to machine appliqué the pieces. Place the stabilizer beneath

the fabric layers and use a small zigzag stitch to sew around each shape, smoothly covering the raw fabric edge. If your machine has stitch options,

use them to detail the appliqués. After the stitching is complete, remove the stabilizer according to the manufacturer's instructions.

# Templates for Maple Leaf Block

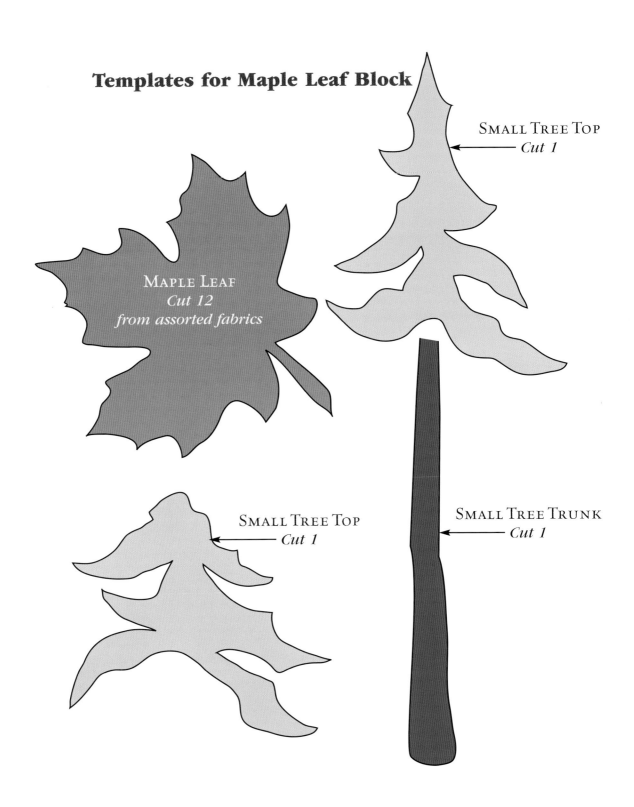

SMALL TREE TOP
*Cut 1*

MAPLE LEAF
*Cut 12*
*from assorted fabrics*

SMALL TREE TOP
*Cut 1*

SMALL TREE TRUNK
*Cut 1*

# Templates for Maple Leaf Block

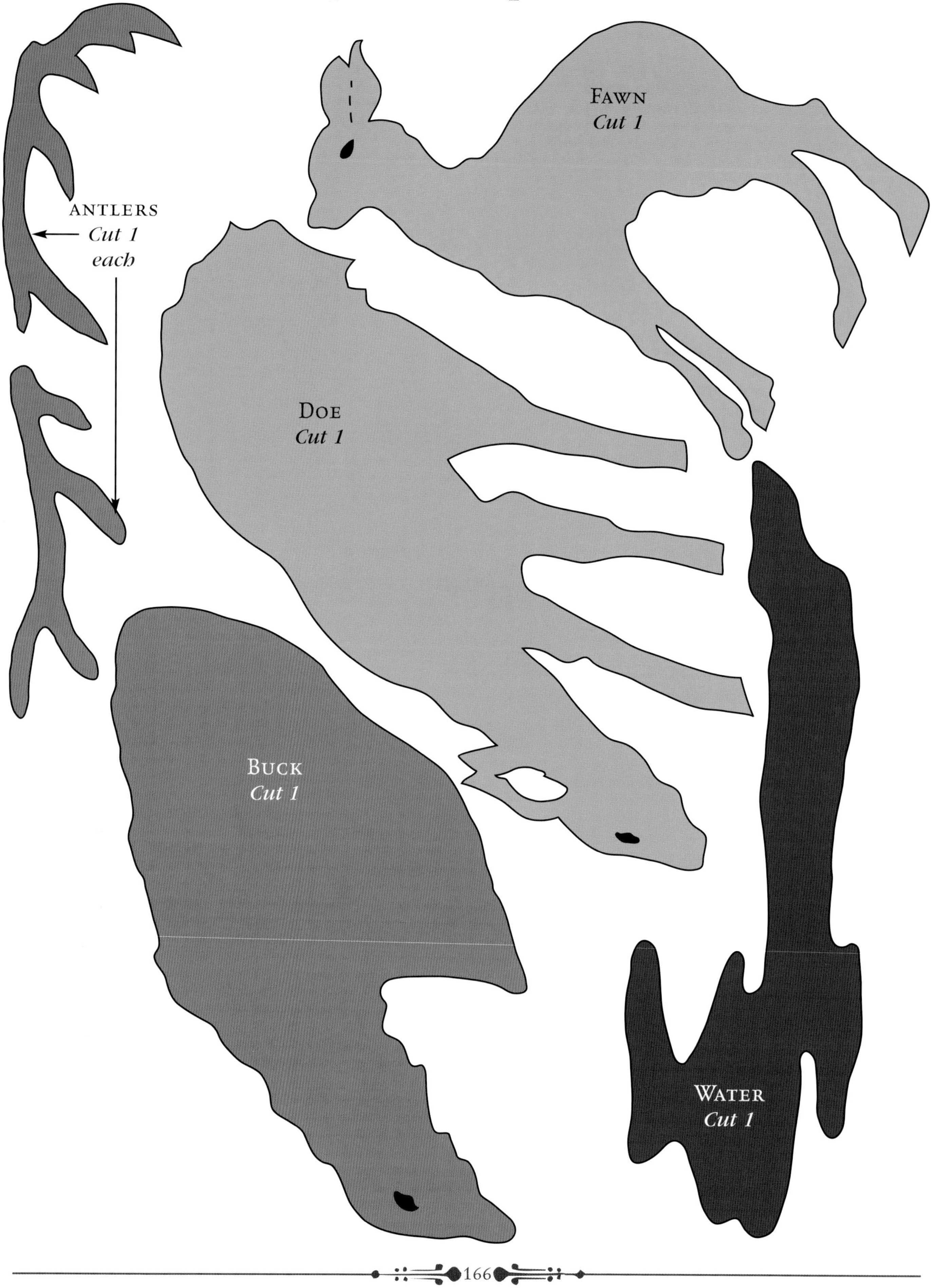

FAWN
*Cut 1*

ANTLERS
*Cut 1
each*

DOE
*Cut 1*

BUCK
*Cut 1*

WATER
*Cut 1*

# Templates for Maple Leaf Block

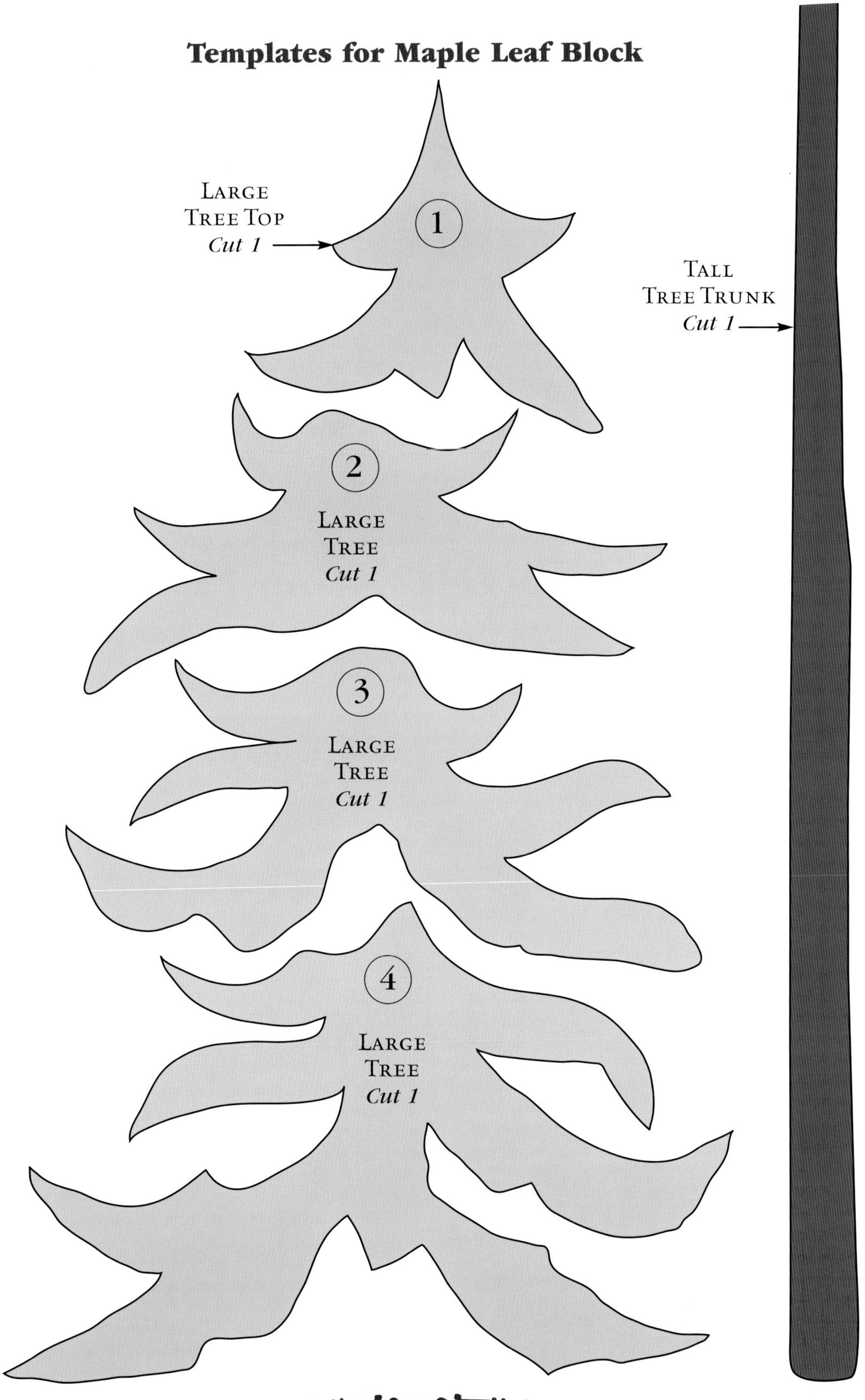

LARGE
TREE TOP
*Cut 1*

1

LARGE
TREE
*Cut 1*

2

3

LARGE
TREE
*Cut 1*

4

LARGE
TREE
*Cut 1*

TALL
TREE TRUNK
*Cut 1*

# Quilt it Quick

# Maple Leaf Wallhanging

## Materials

*Finished size is approximately 33" x 33"*

Refer to the general instructions on pages 6-7 before starting this project.

*Fabrics are based on 42"-wide cotton fabric that has not been washed.*

1 completed Maple Leaf block

1/4 yard of dark brown fabric for cornerstones

1/4 yard of burnt orange fabric for sashing

1 yard of dark green fabric for borders and binding

43" x 43" piece of batting

43" x 43" piece of fabric for backing

## Cutting Instructions

- From the dark brown fabric, cut:
  1 strip 2-1/2" x 42"; from this strip, cut:
      4 squares 2-1/2" x 2-1/2"

- From the burnt orange fabric cut:
  2 strips 2-1/2" x 42"; from these strips, cut:
      4 rectangles 2-1/2" x 21-1/2"

- From dark green fabric, cut:
  4 strips 4-1/2" x 42"
  5 strips 2-1/2" x 42"

## Assembling the Wallhanging

1. Sew a burnt orange 2-1/2" x 21-1/2" rectangle on each side of the Maple Leaf block. Press toward the block.

2. Sew a dark brown 2-1/2" x 2-1/2" square on each end of 2 burnt orange 2-1/2" x 21-1/2" rectangles. Press toward the dark brown.

*Make 2*

3. Sew rectangles from Step 2 to the top and bottom of the Maple Leaf block. Press in the direction of least amount of bulk.

4. Measure the width of the wallhanging through the center to get top and bottom border measurement. Cut two strips to that length from the dark green 4-1/2"-wide strips. Sew strips to the top and bottom. Press toward the border.

5. Measure the length of the wallhanging through the center to get side border measurement. Cut two dark green strips to that length from the 4-1/2"-wide strips. Sew to each side. Press toward the border.

## Finishing the Wallhanging

1. Layer the backing fabric, batting, and wallhanging top.

2. Hand or machine quilt as desired.

3. Finish the wallhanging by sewing on the binding.

# Horizon Block

*Sky meets water in a block with patterns for an appliqué
scene that captures the essence of every fisherman's dream—
taking the day off with nothing to do but fish!*

## Materials

*Finished size is approximately 21" x 21"*

Refer to the general instructions on pages 6-7 before starting this project.

*Fabrics are based on 42"-wide cotton fabric that has not been washed.*

3/8 yard of light blue fabric for background

∎

1/2 yard of dark blue fabric for background

∎

1/4 yard of light green fabric for line of trees

∎

Scraps of medium blue and aqua fabric for water ripples

∎

Scraps of brown fabric for canoe ribs, eagle wings, hair, and pants

∎

Scrap of dark red fabric for canoe

∎

Scraps of golden brown fabric for inside canoe and net handle

∎

Scraps of light brown fabric for paddle and belt

∎

Scraps of tan fabric for net

∎

Scraps of off-white fabric for eagle head, face, and arm

∎

Scraps of green fabric for sleeve, shirt, and fish

∎

1 yard of fusible web

∎

Stabilizer for appliqués

∎

Sulky® threads to match appliqué fabrics

# Horizon Block

## Cutting Instructions

*(A 1/4" seam allowance is included in these measurements.)*

• From the light blue fabric, cut:

1 strip 10" x 42"; from this strip, cut:

1 rectangle 10" x 21-1/2"

• From the dark blue fabric, cut:

1 strip 12" x 42"; from this strip, cut:

1 rectangle 12" x 21-1/2"

## Assembling the Block

1. Sew the light blue 10" x 21-1/2" rectangle to the dark blue 12" x 21-1/2" rectangle.

2. Press toward the dark blue.

## Adding the Appliqués

1. Trace all appliqué templates from pages 172-175 and cut out.

2. Refer to general instructions to prepare pieces for appliqué.

3. Use lightweight tear-away stabilizer to machine appliqué the pieces. Place the stabilizer beneath the fabric layers and use a small zigzag stitch to sew around each shape, smoothly covering the raw fabric edge. If your machine has stitch options, use them to detail the appliqués. After the stitching is complete, remove the stabilizer according to the manufacturer's instructions.

## TREES
*Cut 1*

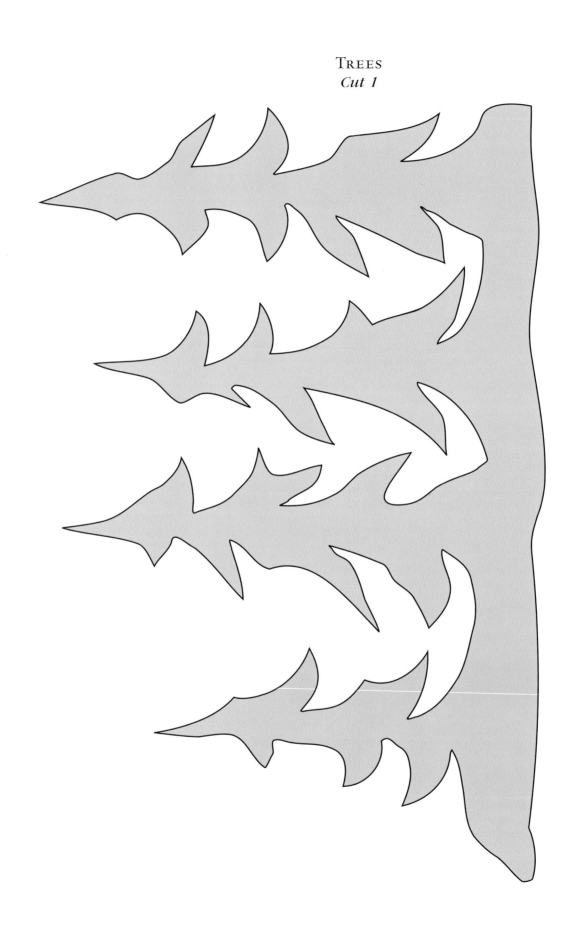

TREES
*Cut 1*

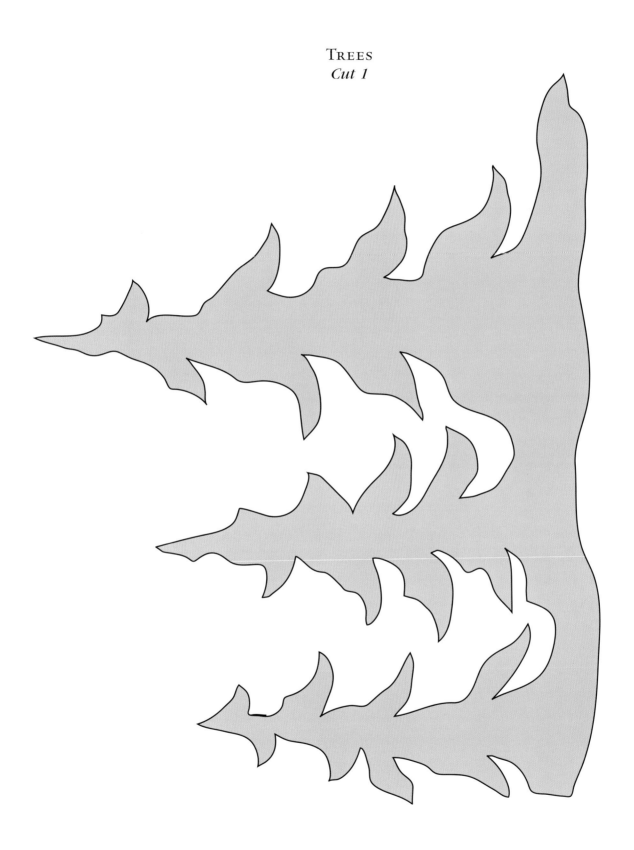

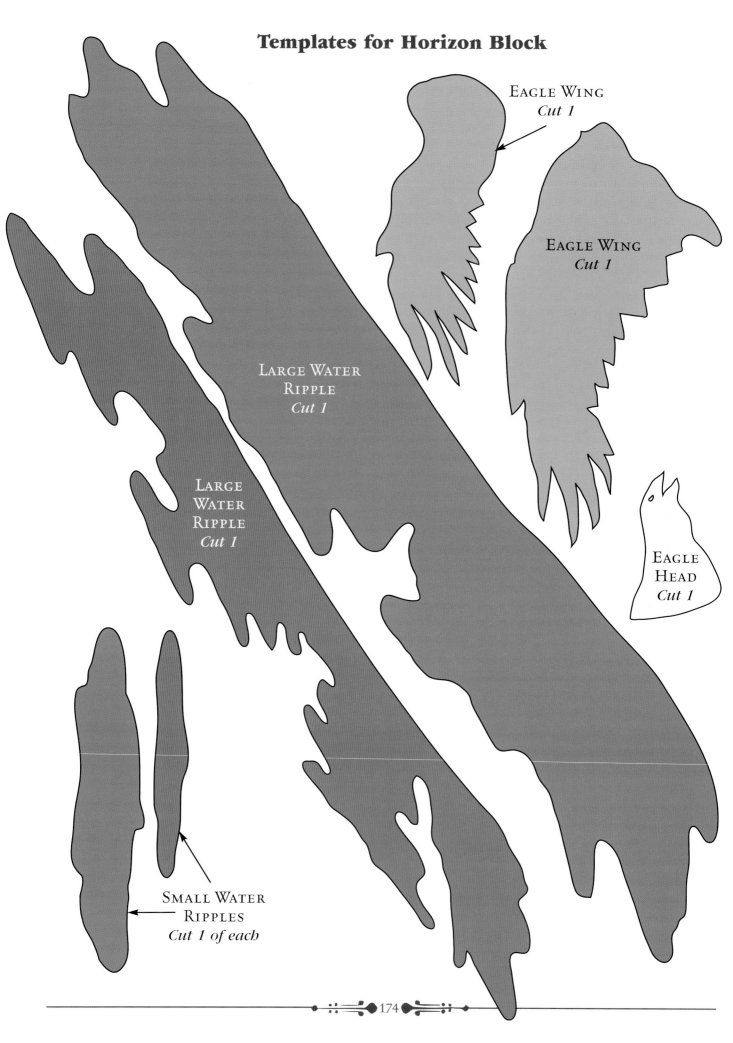

# Templates for Horizon Block

EAGLE WING
*Cut 1*

EAGLE WING
*Cut 1*

LARGE WATER
RIPPLE
*Cut 1*

LARGE
WATER
RIPPLE
*Cut 1*

EAGLE
HEAD
*Cut 1*

SMALL WATER
RIPPLES
*Cut 1 of each*

# Templates for Horizon Block

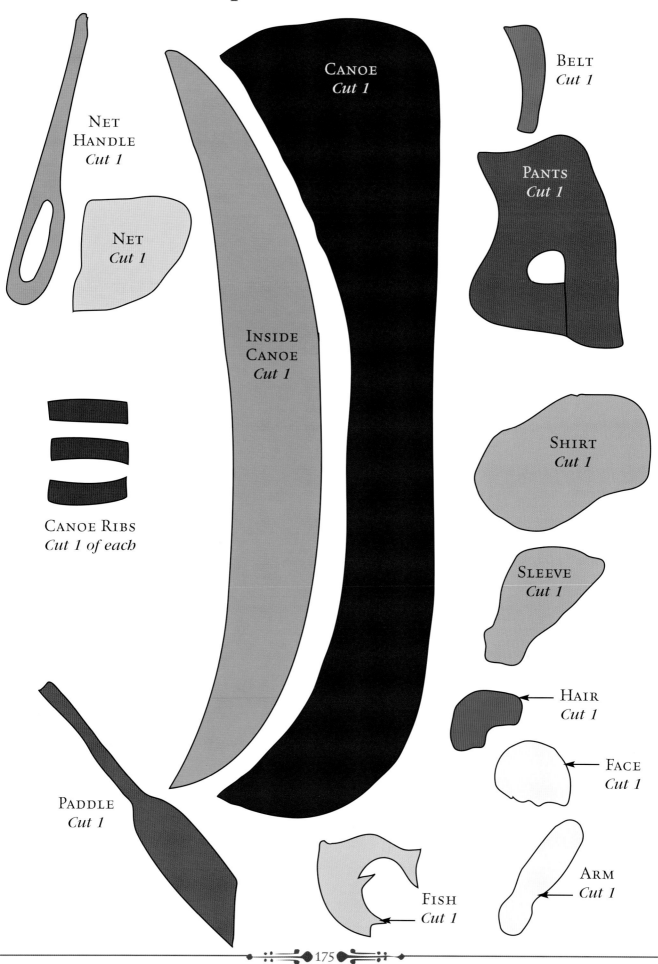

**NET HANDLE** *Cut 1*

**NET** *Cut 1*

**CANOE RIBS** *Cut 1 of each*

**INSIDE CANOE** *Cut 1*

**CANOE** *Cut 1*

**BELT** *Cut 1*

**PANTS** *Cut 1*

**SHIRT** *Cut 1*

**SLEEVE** *Cut 1*

**HAIR** *Cut 1*

**FACE** *Cut 1*

**ARM** *Cut 1*

**PADDLE** *Cut 1*

**FISH** *Cut 1*

The old-fashioned Butterfly block brings the meadow to life with appliqué patterns for colorful blooms, butterflies, and a hummingbird on a wildflower wallhanging and pillows.

## Materials

**Finished size is approximately 21" x 21"**

Refer to the general instructions on pages 6-7
before starting this project.

*Fabrics are based on 42"-wide
cotton fabric that has not been washed.*

1/2 yard of pale yellow fabric for background

1/3 yard of golden brown fabric for background

1/3 yard total of 3 assorted green fabrics for
leaves, wildflower stems, wings, body, and tail

Scraps of purple fabric for wildflowers

Scraps of periwinkle fabric for tree blossoms

Scraps of yellow, orange, gold and black fabric
for butterflies and hummingbird's beak

Scrap of red fabric for hummingbird's head

Scrap of brown fabric for branch

1-1/2 yards of fusible web

Stabilizer for appliqués

Sulky® threads to match appliqué fabrics

## Butterfly Block

### Cutting Instructions

*(A 1/4" seam allowance is included in these measurements.)*

• From the pale yellow fabric, cut:
  1 strip 5-3/4" x 42"; from this strip, cut:
      4 squares 5-3/4" x 5-3/4"
  1 strip 6-1/8" x 42"; from this strip, cut:
      6 squares 6-1/8" x 6-1/8"; cut squares in half
      diagonally to make 12 half-square triangles

• From the golden brown fabric, cut:
  1 strip 6-1/8" x 42"; from this strip, cut
      6 squares 6-1/8" x 6-1/8"; cut squares in half
      diagonally to make 12 half-square triangles

## Assembling the Block

1. Sew a pale yellow 6-1/8" half-square triangle and a golden brown 6-1/8" half-square triangle together to make 1 Unit A. Press toward the golden brown. You will need 12 Unit A.

*Unit A; Make 12*

2. Sew 2 Unit A together to make 1 Unit B. Press in the direction of least amount of bulk. You will need 4 Unit B.

*Unit B; Make 4*

3. Sew 2 Unit A together to make 1 Unit C. Press in the direction of least amount of bulk. You will need 2 Unit C.

*Unit C; Make 2*

4. Sew a pale yellow 5-3/4" square on each end of a Unit C to make 1 Unit D. Press toward the square. You will need 2 Unit D.

*Unit D; Make 2*

5. Sew 4 Unit B together to make 1 Unit E. Press in the direction of least amount of bulk. You will need 1 Unit E.

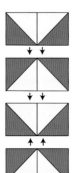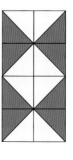

*Unit E; Make 1*

6. Sew a Unit D to each side of Unit E. Press in the direction of least amount of bulk.

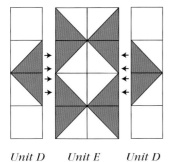

Unit D     Unit E     Unit D

*Adding the Appliqués*

1. Trace all appliqué templates from pages 178 - 181 and cut out.

2. Refer to general instructions to prepare pieces for appliqué.

3. Use lightweight tear-away stabilizer to machine appliqué the pieces. Place the stabilizer beneath the fabric layers and use a small zigzag stitch to sew around each shape, smoothly covering the raw fabric edge. If your machine has stitch options, use them to detail the appliqués. After the stitching is complete, remove the stabilizer according to the manufacturer's instructions.

## Templates for Butterfly Block

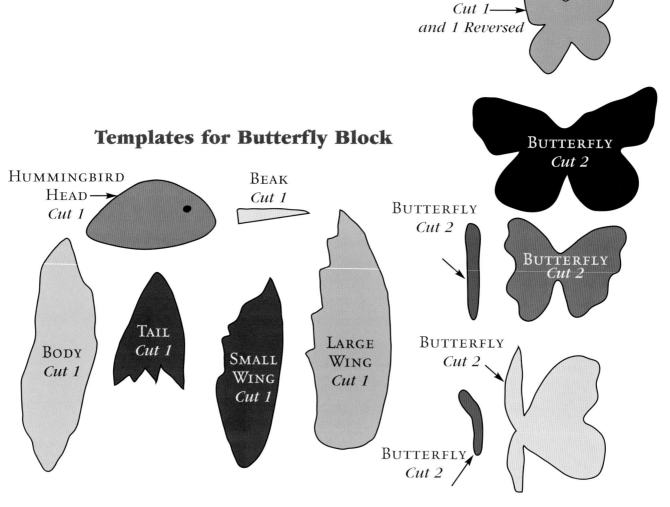

BUTTERFLY
Cut 1⟶
and 1 Reversed

BUTTERFLY
Cut 2

BUTTERFLY
Cut 2

BUTTERFLY
Cut 2

BUTTERFLY
Cut 2

BUTTERFLY
Cut 2

HUMMINGBIRD
HEAD⟶
Cut 1

BEAK
Cut 1

BODY
Cut 1

TAIL
Cut 1

SMALL
WING
Cut 1

LARGE
WING
Cut 1

# Templates for Butterfly Block

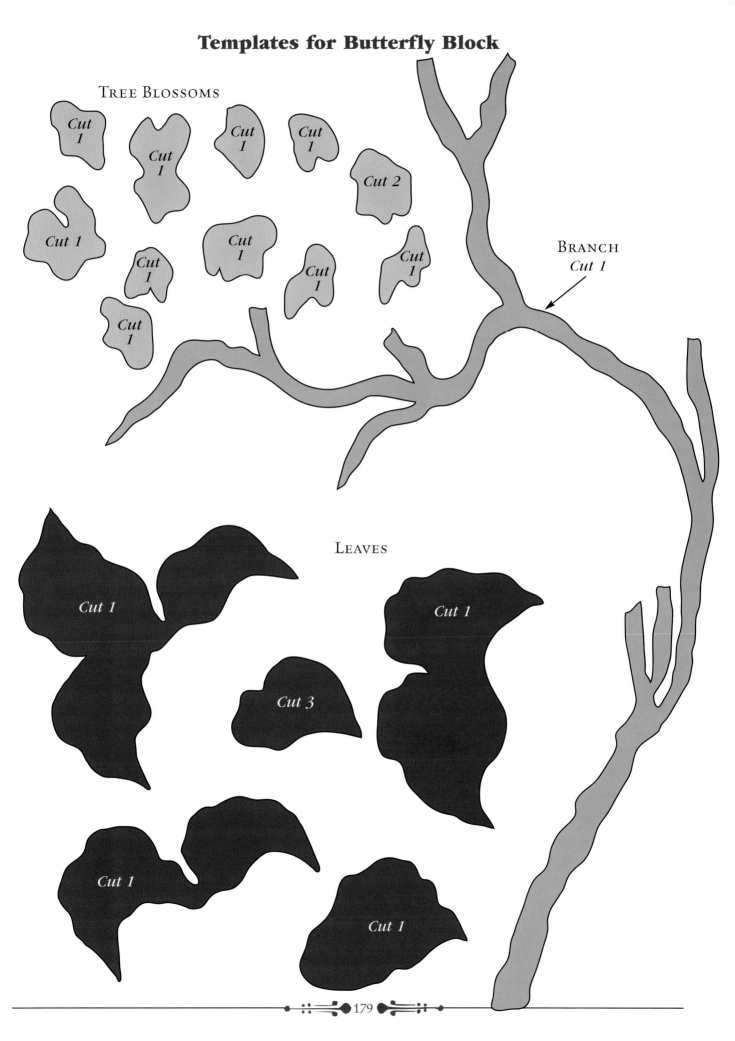

Tree Blossoms

Cut 1
Cut 1
Cut 1
Cut 1
Cut 2
Cut 1
Cut 1
Cut 1
Cut 1
Cut 1
Cut 1

Branch
Cut 1

Leaves

Cut 1
Cut 1
Cut 3
Cut 1
Cut 1

# Templates for Butterfly Block

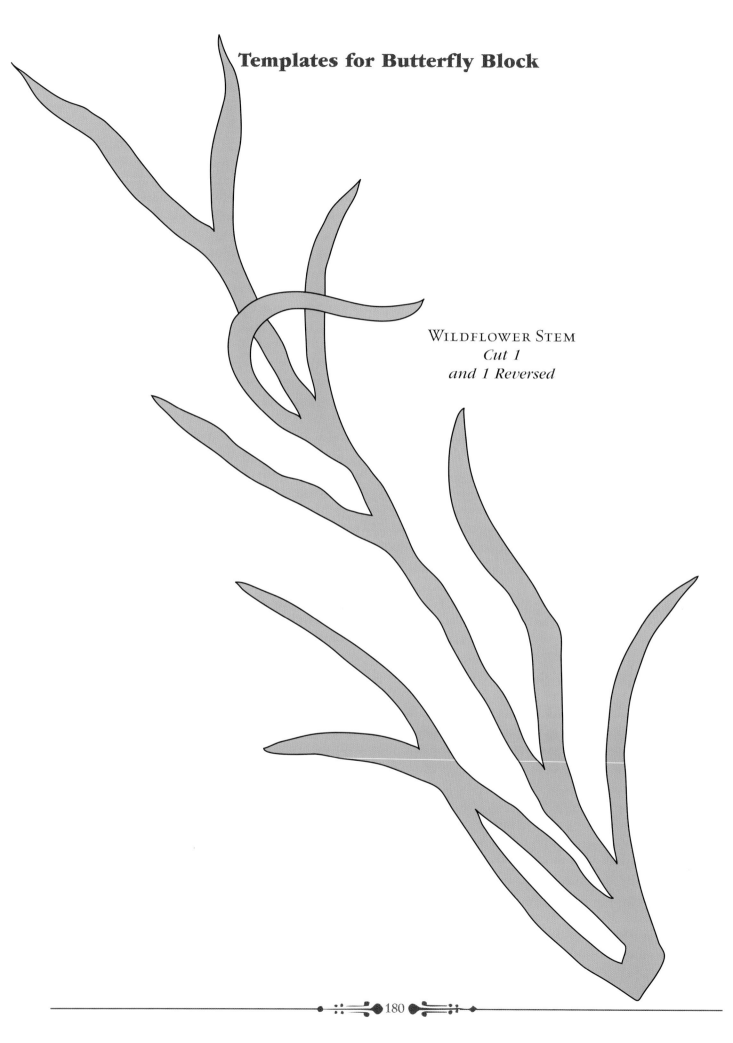

WILDFLOWER STEM
*Cut 1
and 1 Reversed*

# Templates for Butterfly Block

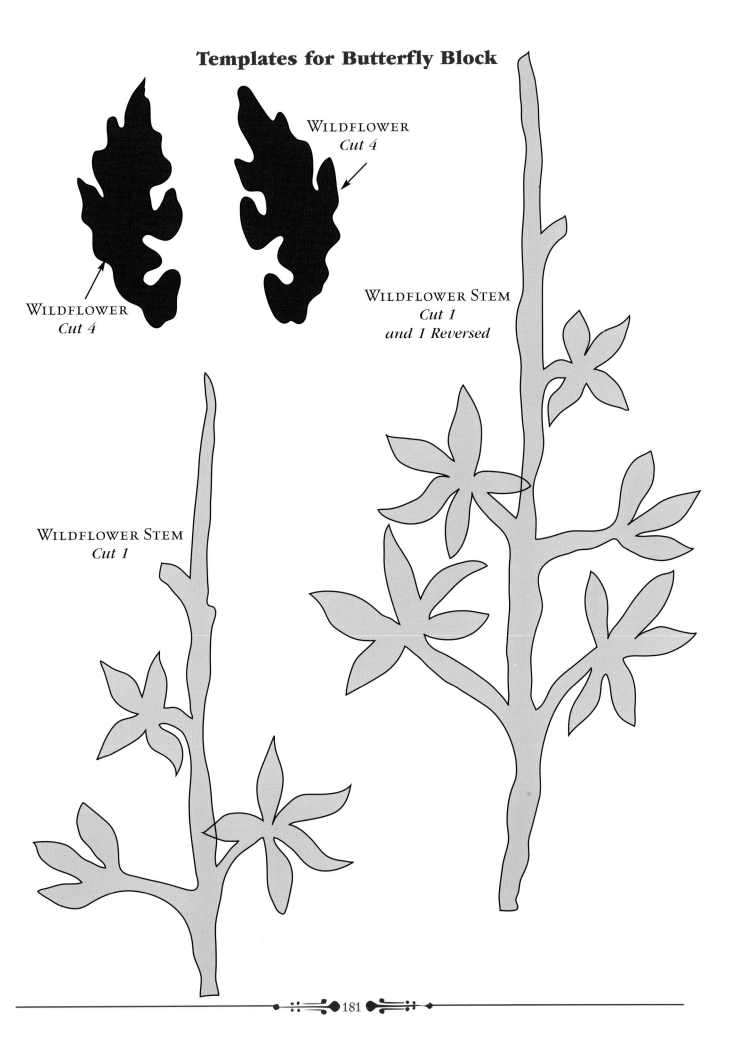

WILDFLOWER
*Cut 4*

WILDFLOWER
*Cut 4*

WILDFLOWER STEM
*Cut 1
and 1 Reversed*

WILDFLOWER STEM
*Cut 1*

# Butterfly Wallhanging

## Materials

*Finished size is approximately 33" x 33"*

Refer to the general instructions on pages 6-7 before starting this project.

*Fabrics are based on 42"-wide cotton fabric that has not been washed.*

One completed Butterfly Block

Scraps of dark green fabric for cornerstones

1/3 yard of purple fabric for sashing

1 yard of pale yellow fabric for borders and binding

43" x 43" piece of batting

43" x 43" piece of fabric for backing

## Cutting Instructions

• From the dark green fabric, cut:
   4 squares 2-1/2" x 2-1/2" for cornerstones

• From the purple fabric, cut:
   4 strips 2-1/2" x 42"; from these strips, cut:
      4 rectangles 2-1/2" x 21-1/2" for sashing

• From the pale yellow fabric, cut:
   4 strips 4-1/2" x 42" for border
   5 strips 2-1/2" x 42" for binding

## Assembling the Wallhanging

1. Sew a purple 2-1/2" x 21-1/2" rectangle on each side of the Butterfly block.

2. Sew a dark green 2-1/2" x 2-1/2" square on each end of 2 purple 2-1/2" x 21-1/2" rectangles. Press toward the dark green.

*Make 2*

3. Sew rectangles from Step 2 to the top and bottom of the Butterfly block. Press in the direction of least amount of bulk.

4. Measure the width of the wallhanging through the center to get top and bottom border measurement. Cut two strips that length from the purple 4-1/2"- wide strips. Sew strips to the top and bottom. Press toward the border.

5. Measure the length of the wallhanging through the center to get side border measurement. Cut two pale yellow strips that length from the 4-1/2" wide strips. Sew strips to each side. Press toward the border.

## Finishing the Wallhanging

1. Layer the backing fabric, batting, and wallhanging top.

2. Hand or machine quilt as desired.

3. Finish the wallhanging by sewing on the binding.

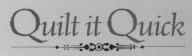

## Pillows

### Materials

*Refer to the general instructions on pages 6-7 before starting this project.*

***Finished size is approximately 17" x 17" for large pillow and 10" x 10" for small pillow***

1 yard of cream fabric for pillow backgrounds; outer border and backing of large pillow

■

1/4 yard of purple fabric for inner border of large pillow

■

1/3 yard of teal fabric for borders and back of small pillow

■

16" x 16" pillow form for large pillow and fiberfill for small pillow

■

Scraps of light green, black, yellow, red, dark and light purple fabric for wildflower stems, butterflies, hummingbird, and wildflowers

■

1/2 yard of fusible webbing

■

12" x 12" piece of batting for large pillow

■

Sulky® threads to match appliqué fabrics

## Butterfly Pillow

### Cutting Instructions

• From the cream fabric, cut:
  10" x 10" square for background
  2 strips 3" x 42" for outer border

• From the purple fabric, cut:
  2 strips 2" x 42"; from these strips, cut:
    2 strips 2" x 10" for inner border

### Adding the Appliqués

1. Trace appliqué templates on pages 178 and 181 and cut out.

2. Refer to general instructions to prepare pieces for appliqué.

3. Use lightweight tear-away stabilizer to machine appliqué the pieces. Place the stabilizer beneath the fabric layers and use a small zigzag stitch to sew around each shape, smoothly covering the raw fabric edge. If your machine has stitch options, use them to detail the appliqués. After the stitching is complete, remove the stabilizer according to the manufacturer's instructions.

### Assembling the Pillow

1. Sew a 2" x 10" purple strip to the top and bottom of pillow center. Press toward the outside. Measure sides of pillow and cut 2 strips of purple fabric to that measurement and sew to sides.

2. Measure the width of the pillow top through the center. Cut 2 strips of 3"-wide cream fabric to that measurement and sew to top and bottom. Press toward the outside. Measure pillow through the center lengthwise. Cut 2 strips to that measurement and sew to the sides of the pillow.

3. To machine quilt the pillow top, layer batting and pillow top. Quilt as desired.

4. Press and trim excess batting from the pillow top. Layer pillow backing right side up and pillow top wrong side up. Stitch 1/4" seam around pillow top, leaving an opening at bottom to insert pillow form or stuffing. Clip corners and any excess backing fabric. Turn. Insert pillow form and stitch opening closed.

## Hummingbird Pillow

### Cutting Instructions

• From the cream fabric, cut:
  6-1/2" x 6-1/2" square

• From the teal fabric, cut:
  1 strip 2-1/2" x 42" for border
    2 rectangles 2-1/2" x 6-1/2"
    2 rectangles 2-1/2" x 10-1/2"

### Assembling the Pillow

Refer to Steps 2-4 for the Butterfly Pillow, eliminating sashing and quilting.

# DELECTABLE MOUNTAIN BLOCK

Standing the test of time, the Delectable Mountain block rises majestically in an 8-block snuggler and as the background of an appliqué scene featuring the Granola Girl® on a hike for a better view.

## Materials

*Finished size is approximately 21" x 21"*

Refer to the general instructions on pages 6-7 before starting this project.

*Fabrics are based on 42"-wide cotton fabric that has not been washed.*

1/2 yard of tan fabric for background

1/2 yard of teal fabric for background

2/3 yard of dark purple fabric for background

1/4 yard total of medium green fabric for trees

1/8 yard of light brown fabric for tree trunks and moose antlers

1/4 yard of dark brown fabric for hiking path

Scraps of light blue fabric for clouds

Scraps of fabric for moose, hair, face, hand, legs, cap, walking stick, shirt, shorts, and boots

3/4 yard of fusible web

Stabilizer for appliqués

Sulky® threads to match appliqué fabrics

# Delectable Mountain Block

## Cutting Instructions

*(A 1/4" seam allowance is included in these measurements.)*

• From the tan fabric, cut:
  1 strip 4-5/8" x 42"; from this strip, cut:
    4 squares 4-5/8" x 4-5/8"; cut squares in half diagonally to make 8 half-square triangles
    *Note: 1 half-square triangle will not be used.*
  1 strip 8-5/8" x 42"; from this strip, cut:
    1 square 8-5/8" x 8-5/8"; cut square in half diagonally to make 2 half-square triangles

• From the teal fabric, cut:
  1 strip 8-1/2" x 42"; from this strip, cut:
    1 rectangle 8-1/2" x 21-1/2"
  1 strip 4-5/8" x 42"; from this strip, cut:
    4 squares 4-5/8" x 4-5/8"; cut squares in half diagonally to make 8 triangles

• From the dark purple fabric, cut:
  1 strip 15-5/8" x 42"; from this strip, cut:
    1 square 15-5/8" x 15-5/8"; cut square in half diagonally to make 2 half-square triangles
  *Note: 1 half-square triangle will not be used.*

## Assembling the Block

1. Sew a tan 4-5/8" half-square triangle and a teal 4-5/8" half-square triangle together to make 1 Unit A. Press toward the teal. You will need 6 Unit A.

Unit A;
Make 6

2. Sew 3 Unit A together as shown to make 1 Unit B. Press in the direction of least amount of bulk.

Unit B; Make 1

3. Sew a tan 4-5/8" half-square triangle to the left side of Unit B, as shown to make 1 Unit C. Press toward the tan triangle, carefully.

*Unit C; Make 1*

4. Sew a teal 4-5/8" half-square triangle to the right side of Unit C, as shown to make 1 Unit D. Press toward the teal triangle, carefully.

*Unit D; Make 1*

5. Sew 3 Unit A together, as shown to make 1 Unit E. Press in the direction of least amount of bulk.

*Unit E; Make 1*

6. Sew a teal 4-5/8" half-square triangle to the left side of Unit E, as shown to make 1 Unit F. Press toward the teal triangle, carefully.

*Unit F; Make 1*

7. Sew Unit F to the left side of the purple 15-5/8" half-square triangle, as shown to make 1 Unit G. Press toward the purple triangle, carefully.

 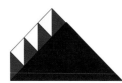

*Unit G; Make 1*

8. Sew Unit D to the right side of Unit G, as shown to make 1 Unit H. Press toward the purple triangle, carefully.

*Unit H; Make 1*

9. Sew a tan 8-5/8" half-square triangle to each side of Unit H, as shown to make 1 Unit I. Press toward the tan triangle, carefully.

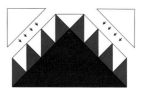 

*Unit I; Make 1*

10. Sew the 8-1/2" x 21-1/2" teal rectangle to Unit I, as shown. Press toward the rectangle, carefully.

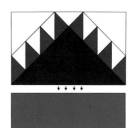 

11. Square up the block, if necessary. Leave a 1/4" seam allowance past the intersection and make sure the corners are at 90-degree angles.

*1/4" seam allowance past intersection*

## Adding the Appliqués

1. Trace all appliqué templates from pages 189 - 191 and cut out.

2. Refer to general instructions to prepare pieces for appliqué.

3. Use lightweight tear-away stabilizer to machine appliqué the pieces. Place the stabilizer beneath the fabric layers and use a small zigzag stitch to sew around each shape, smoothly covering the raw fabric edge. If your machine has stitch options, use them to detail the appliqués. After the stitching is complete, remove the stabilizer according to the manufacturer's instructions.

# Templates for Delectable Mountain Block

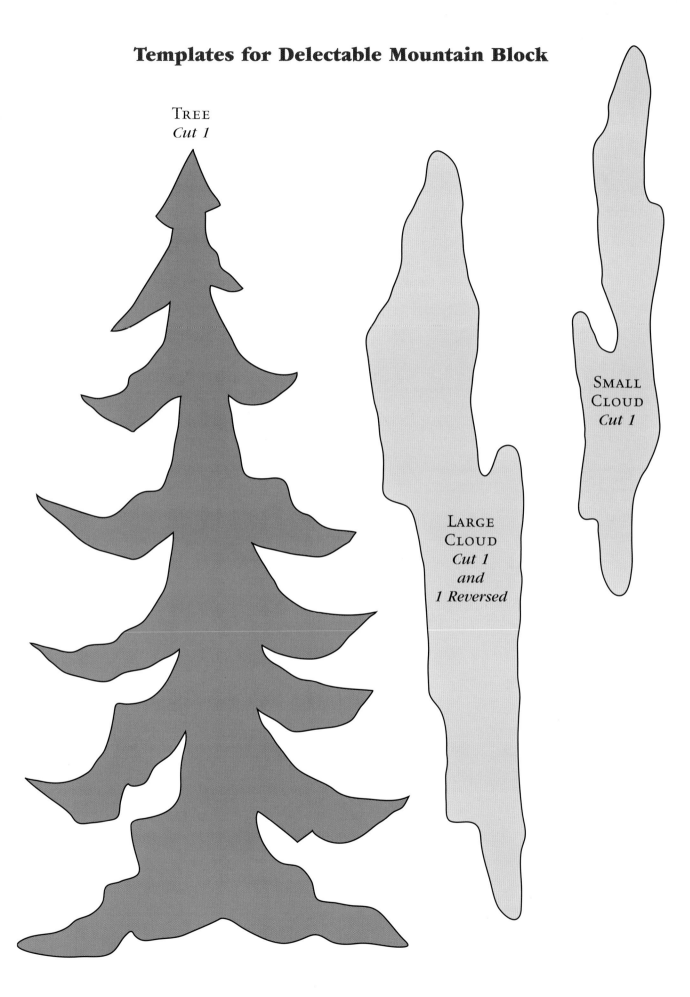

TREE
*Cut 1*

LARGE
CLOUD
*Cut 1
and
1 Reversed*

SMALL
CLOUD
*Cut 1*

# Templates for Delectable Mountain Block

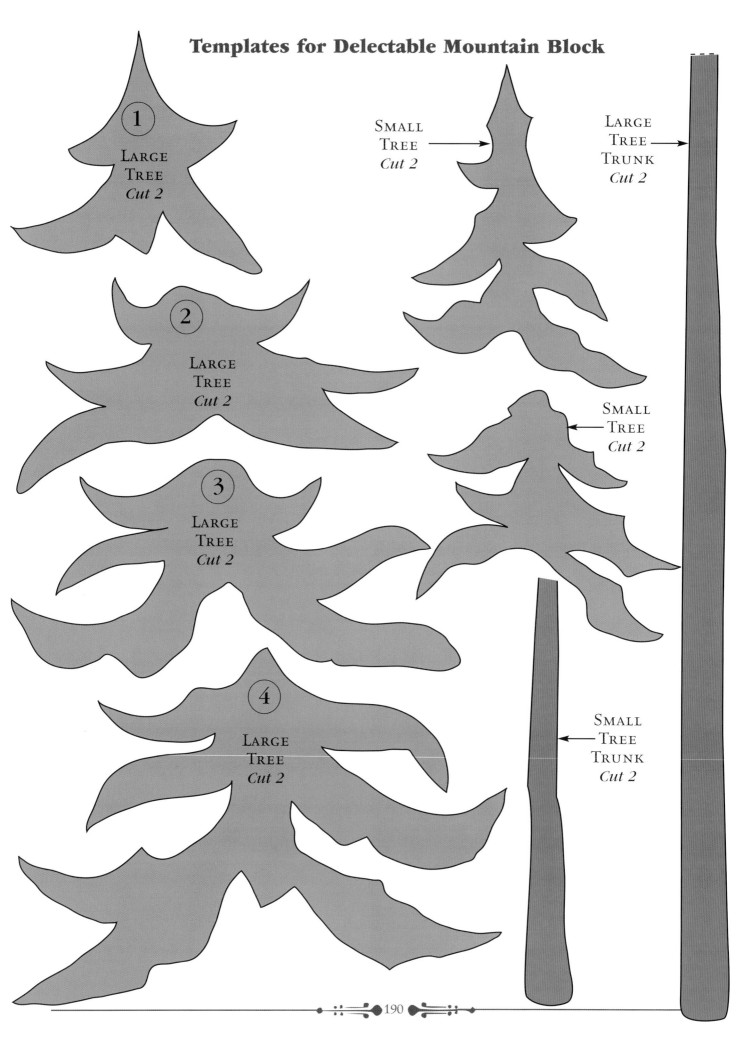

① LARGE
TREE
*Cut 2*

② LARGE
TREE
*Cut 2*

③ LARGE
TREE
*Cut 2*

④ LARGE
TREE
*Cut 2*

SMALL
TREE
*Cut 2*

SMALL
TREE
*Cut 2*

LARGE
TREE
TRUNK
*Cut 2*

SMALL
TREE
TRUNK
*Cut 2*

# Templates for Delectable Mountain Block

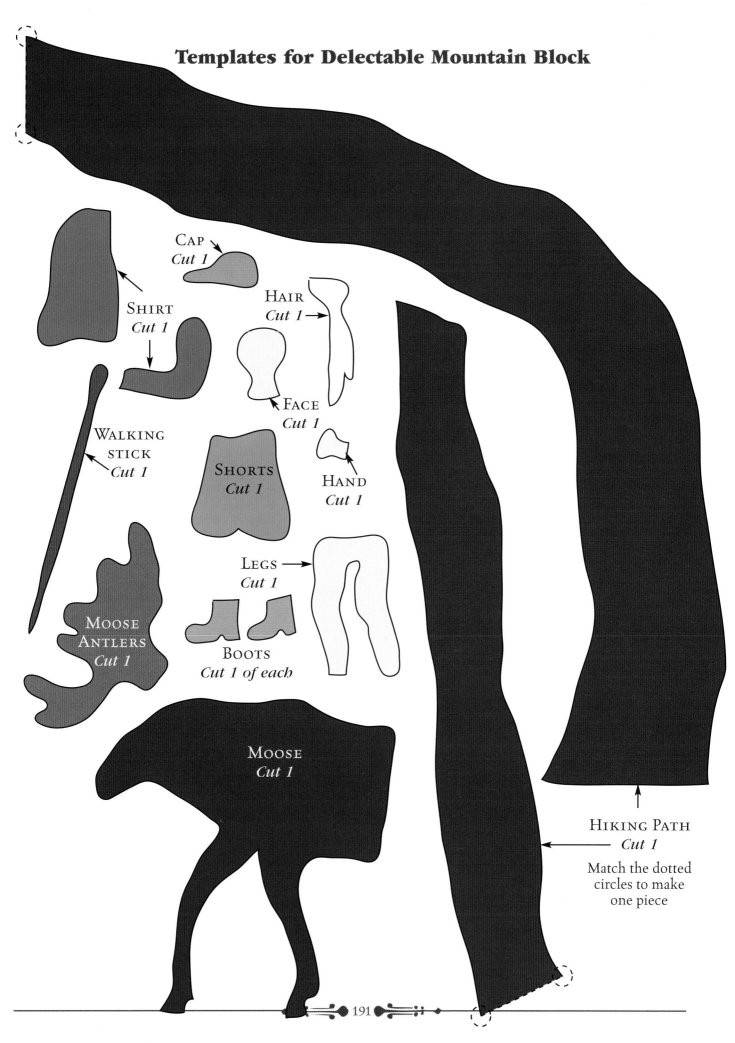

CAP
*Cut 1*

SHIRT
*Cut 1*

HAIR
*Cut 1*

FACE
*Cut 1*

WALKING
stick
*Cut 1*

SHORTS
*Cut 1*

HAND
*Cut 1*

LEGS
*Cut 1*

MOOSE
ANTLERS
*Cut 1*

BOOTS
*Cut 1 of each*

MOOSE
*Cut 1*

HIKING PATH
*Cut 1*

Match the dotted
circles to make
one piece

# DELECTABLE MOUNTAIN SNUGGLER

## Delectable Mountain Blocks

Make 8 Blocks

### Cutting Instructions

*(A 1/4" seam allowance is included in these measurements.)*

- From the pale lavender fabric, cut:

  3 strips 4-7/8" x 42"; from these strips, cut:

  20 squares 4-7/8" x 4-7/8"; cut squares

  diagonally in half to make 40 half-square triangles

  2 strips 6-5/8" x 42"; from these strips, cut:

  8 squares 6-5/8" x 6-5/8"; cut squares diagonally

  to make 16 half-square triangles

- From the medium purple fabric, cut:

  3 strips 4-7/8" x 42"; from these strips, cut:

  24 squares 4-7/8" x 4-7/8"; cut squares

  diagonally to make 48 half-square triangles

- From the dark purple fabric, cut:

  2 strips 3-1/2" x 42"; from these strips, cut:

  15 squares 3-1/2" x 3-1/2" for cornerstones

  2 strips 12-7/8" x 42"; from these strips, cut:

  4 squares 12-7/8" x 12-7/8"; cut squares

  diagonally to make 8 half-square triangles

  1 strip 6-7/8" x 42"; from this strip, cut:

  2 squares 6-7/8" x 6-7/8"; cut these squares

  diagonally to make 4 half-square triangles

- From the lavender fabric, cut:

  7 strips 6-1/2" x 42" for inner border

- From the medium teal fabric, cut:

  9 strips 3-1/2" x 42"; from these strips, cut:

  10 rectangles 3-1/2" x 17-3/4"

  12 rectangles 3-1/2" x 11-3/4"

• From the dark teal fabric, cut:

　1 strip 6-7/8" x 42"; from these strips, cut:

　　2 squares 6-7/8" x 6-7/8"; cut these squares diagonally to make 4 half-square triangles

　8 strips 3-1/2" x 42" for outer border

　7 strips 3" x 42" for binding

## Assembling the Block

1. Sew a pale lavender 4-7/8" triangle and a medium purple 4-7/8" triangle together to make 1 Unit A. Press toward the medium purple. You will need 32 Unit A.

Unit A;
Make 32

2. Sew 2 Unit A together, as shown to make 1 Unit B. Press in the direction of least amount of bulk. You will need 8 Unit B.

Unit B; Make 8

3. Sew a pale lavender 4-7/8" triangle to the left side of a Unit B to make 1 unit C. Press toward the pale lavender. You will need 8 Unit C.

Unit C; Make 8

4. Sew a medium purple 4-7/8" triangle to the right side of a Unit C, as shown to make 1 Unit D. Press toward the medium purple triangle. You will have 8 Unit D.

Unit D; Make 8

5. Sew 2 Unit A together, as shown to make 1 Unit E. Press in the direction of least amount of bulk. You will need 8 Unit E.

Unit E; Make 8

6. Sew a medium purple 4-7/8" triangle to the left side of a Unit E, as shown to make 1 unit F. Press toward the medium purple triangle. You will need 8 Unit F.

Unit F; Make 8

7. Sew a Unit F to the left side of each of the dark purple 12-7/8" triangle, as shown to make 1 Unit G. Press toward the dark. You will need 8 Unit G.

Unit G; Make 8

8. Sew a Unit D to the right side of a Unit G, as shown to make 1 Unit H. Press toward the dark. You will need 8 Unit H.

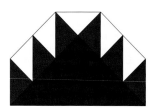

Unit H; Make 8

9. Sew a pale lavender 6-5/8" triangle on each side of Unit H, as shown to make 1 Unit I. Press toward the pale lavender. You will need 8 Unit I.

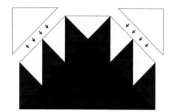 

*Unit I; Make 8*

10. Square up the block, if necessary. Leave a 1/4" seam allowance past the intersection and make sure the corners are 90-degree angles.

## Adding the Sashing

1. Sew 3 dark purple 3-1/2" squares to 2 medium teal 3-1/2" x 17-3/4" rectangles, as shown to make 1 Unit J. Press toward the medium teal. You will need 5 Unit J.

*Unit J; Make 5*

2. Sew 3 medium teal 3-1/2" x 11-3/4" rectangles and 2 Unit I together, as shown. Press toward the medium teal. You will need 4 rows.

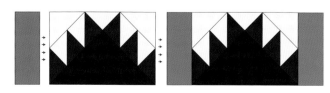

*Make 4 rows*

3. Sew each Unit J and the four rows together, as shown. Press in the direction of least amount of bulk.

## Adding the Borders

1. Sew the 4 dark purple 6-7/8" triangles and the 4 dark teal 6-7/8" triangles together, as shown. Press toward the dark purple. You will have 4 dark purple/dark teal squares.

*Make 4*

2. Measure the width of the quilt top through the center to get top and bottom measurement. Cut 2 strips to that length from the lavender 6-1/2"-wide strips. Set aside.

3. Measure the length of the quilt top through the center to get side measurement. Cut 2 strips that length from the lavender 6-1/2"-wide strips.

4. Sew the dark purple/dark teal squares to each end of the lavender 6-1/2"-wide side border strips, as shown. Press in the direction of least amount of bulk. Set aside.

5. Sew the lavender 6-1/2"-wide inner border strips to the top and bottom of the quilt top. Press toward the dark.

6. Sew the side inner border strips from step 4 to the quilt top. Press toward the dark.

7. Measure the new width of the quilt top through the center to get top and bottom measurement. Cut 2 strips that length from the 3-1/2" dark teal strips. Sew strips to the quilt top and bottom. Press toward the dark.

8. Measure the new length of the quilt top through the center to get side border measurement. Cut 2 strips that length from the 3-1/2" dark teal strips. Sew to the sides of the quilt top. Press toward the dark.

## Finishing the Quilt

1. Layer the backing fabric, batting, and quilt top. Baste the layers together.

2. Hand or machine quilt as desired.

3. Finish the quilt by sewing on the binding.

**Delectable Mountain Snuggler**

The Tree of Life block is the inspiration for a scattering of stars and a forest
of evergreens to appliqué on the block and a woodland wallhanging.

## Materials

*Finished size is approximately 21" x 21"*

Refer to the general instructions on pages 6-7 before starting this project.

*Fabrics are based on 42"-wide cotton fabric that has not been washed.*

2/3 yards of cream fabric for background

1/4 yard of dark green fabric for background

1/2 yard of green fabric for background

1/2 yard of brown fabric for background

Scraps of 3 assorted green fabrics for trees

Scraps of gold fabric for small stars

Scraps of pale yellow fabric for large stars

Scraps of brown fabric for tree trunks

1-1/4 yards of fusible web

Stabilizer for appliqués

Sulky® threads to match appliqué fabrics

## Cutting Instructions

*(A 1/4" seam allowance is included in these measurements.)*

• From the cream fabric, cut:
  1 strip 3-7/8" x 42"; from this strip, cut:
  7 squares 3-7/8" x 3-7/8"; cut these squares in half diagonally to make 14 half-square triangles
  1 strip 3-1/2" x 42"; from this strip, cut:
  2 squares 3-1/2" x 3-1/2"
  1 strip 9-7/8" x 42"; from this strip, cut:
  1 square 9-7/8" x 9-7/8"; cut square in half diagonally to make 2 half-square triangles
  *Note: 1 half-square triangle will not be used.*

• From the dark green fabric, cut:
  1 strip 3-7/8" x 42"; from this strip, cut:
  7 squares 3-7/8" x 3-7/8"; cut squares in half diagonally to make 14 half-square triangles

• From the green fabric, cut:
  1 strip 9-7/8" x 42"; from this strip, cut:
  1 square 9-7/8" x 9-7/8"; cut square in half diagonally to make half-square triangles
  *Note: 1 half-square triangle will not be used.*

• From the brown fabric, cut:
  1 strip 11-1/2" x 42"; from this strip cut:
  2 squares 11-1/2" x 11-1/2"; cut squares in half diagonally to make 4 half-square triangles
  1 rectangle 3/4" x 8 1/2" for tree trunk

## Assembling the Block

1. Sew a cream 3-7/8" half-square triangle and a dark green 3-7/8" half-square triangle together to make 1 Unit A. Press toward the dark green. You will need 14 Unit A.

*Unit A; Make 14*

2. Follow the manufacturer's instructions to fuse web to the wrong side of the 3/4" x 8-1/2" brown rectangle. Trim the rectangle to 5/8" wide. Position the tree trunk in the middle of the cream 9-7/8" half- square triangle and fuse. Machine stitch using a small zigzag down each long edge of the tree trunk. Trim tree trunk off at each raw edge.

3. Sew the appliquéd triangle and the green 9-7/8" half-square triangle together, as shown to make 1 Unit B. Press toward the green.

*Unit B; Make 1*

4. Sew 3 Unit A together, as shown to make 1 Unit C. Press in the direction of least amount of bulk.

*Unit C; Make 1*

5. Sew 3 Unit A together, as shown to make 1 Unit D. Press in direction of least amount of bulk.

*Unit D; Make 1*

6. Sew a cream 3-1/2" square to the left side of Unit C, as shown to make 1 Unit E. Press in the direction of least amount of bulk.

*Unit E; Make 1*

7. Sew Unit D to the left side of Unit B, as shown to make 1 Unit F. Press toward Unit B.

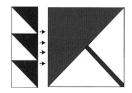 

*Unit F; Make 1*

8. Sew Unit E to the right side of Unit F, as shown to make 1 Unit G. Press toward the large triangle.

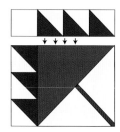 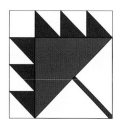

*Unit G; Make 1*

9. Sew 4 Unit A together, as shown to make 1 Unit H. Press in direction of least amount of bulk.

*Unit H; Make 1*

10. Sew 4 Unit A together, as shown to make 1 Unit I. Press in the direction of least amount of bulk.

*Unit I; Make 1*

11. Sew a cream 3-1/2" square to the left side of Unit I, as shown to make 1 Unit J. Press in the direction of least amount of bulk.

*Unit J; Make 1*

12. Sew Unit H to the left side of Unit G, as shown to make 1 Unit K. Press in the direction of least amount of bulk.

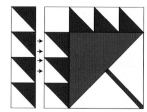 

*Unit K; Make 1*

13. Sew Unit J to Unit K, as shown to make 1 Unit L. Press in the direction of least amount of bulk.

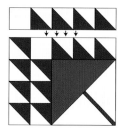 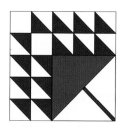

*Unit L; Make 1*

14. Sew 2 brown 11-1/2" half-square triangles on opposite sides of the Unit L block, as shown. Press carefully toward the triangles.

15. Sew the remaining 2 brown 11-1/2" half-square triangles on the opposite sides of the block, as shown. Press carefully toward the triangle. Square up the block, if necessary. Leave a 1/4" seam allowance past the intersection and make sure the corners are at 90-degree angles.

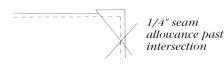

*1/4" seam allowance past intersection*

## Adding the Appliqués

1. Trace all appliqué templates from pages 202-203 and cut out.

2. Refer to general instructions to prepare pieces for appliqué.

3. Use lightweight tear-away stabilizer to machine appliqué the pieces. Place the stabilizer beneath the fabric layers and use a small zigzag stitch to sew around each shape, smoothly covering the raw fabric edge. If your machine has stitch options, use them to detail the appliqués. After the stitching is complete, remove the stabilizer according to the manufacturer's instructions.

# Templates for Tree of Life Block

LARGE
STAR
*Cut 5*

SMALL
STAR
*Cut 6*

LARGE TREE
*Cut 2*

MEDIUM TREE
*Cut 3*

# Templates for Tree of Life Block

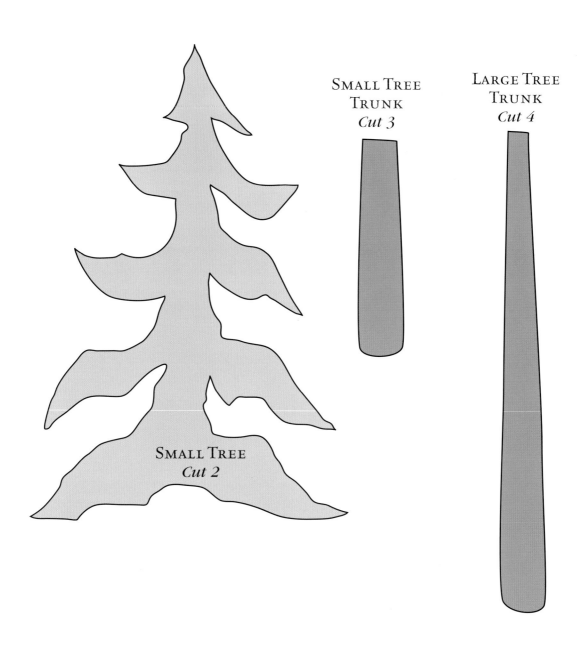

SMALL TREE
TRUNK
*Cut 3*

LARGE TREE
TRUNK
*Cut 4*

SMALL TREE
*Cut 2*

## Tree of Life Wallhanging

### Materials

*Finished size is approximately 33" x 33"*

Refer to the general instructions on pages 6-7 before starting this project.

*Fabrics are based on 42"-wide cotton fabric that has not been washed.*

1 completed Tree of Life block

Scraps of dark brown fabric for cornerstones

1/4 yard of cream fabric for sashing

1/4 yard of green print fabric for borders and binding

43" x 43" piece of batting

43" x 43" piece of backing

## Cutting Instructions

• From the dark brown fabric, cut:
  4 squares 2-1/2" x 2-1/2" for cornerstones

• From the cream fabric, cut:
  2 strips 2-1/2" x 42"; from these strips, cut:
    4 rectangles 2-1/2" x 21-1/2" for sashing

• From the green print fabric, cut:
  4 strips 4-1/2" x 42" for borders
  5 strips 2-1/2" x 42" for binding

## Assembling the Wallhanging

1. Sew a cream 2-1/2" x 21-1/2" rectangle on each side of the Tree of Life block. Press toward the block.

2. Sew a dark brown 2-1/2" x 2-1/2" square on each end of 2 cream 2-1/2" x 21-1/2" rectangles. Press toward the dark brown.

*Make 2*

3. Sew rectangles from Step 2 to the top and bottom of the Tree of Life block. Press in the direction of least amount of bulk.

4. Measure the width of the wallhanging through the center to get top and bottom border measurement. Cut two strips that length from the green print 4-1/2"-wide strips. Sew to the top and bottom. Press toward the border.

5. Measure the length of the wallhanging through the center to get side border measurement. Cut two green print strips that length from the 4-1/2"-wide strips. Sew to each side. Press toward the border.

## Finishing the Wallhanging

1. Layer the backing fabric, batting, and wallhanging top.

2. Hand or machine quilt as desired.

3. Finish the wallhanging by sewing on the binding.

# About
## the Author

Debbie Field, producing her work through Granola Girl® Designs
has emphasized her love of the outdoors in quilts, wallhangings, books,
patterns, accessories, and her own lines of fabric.

Her work is a reflection of her personal experiences since childhood with the
breathtaking sights of nature and wildlife of the great northern woods.

She attributes her outdoor spirit to the warmth of her family and
living an adventurous outdoor lifestyle—a tradition instilled by her parents
and continued with her husband and her sons and their families.

# Acknowledgements

A huge thank you to my creative team. It takes a team to
produce a great book like this. Thank you to each of you for your individual talents:

Sue Longeville

Delores Farmer

Sue Carter

Amy Gutzman

Sharon Saunders

Cindy Kujawa

Kathy Geis

Suzy Peterson

Visit your local quilt shop and ask for Granola Girl® Designs
manufactured by Troy Corporation. Fabric collections used to make projects in this
book include *Marblecake Basics*, *Alpine Years Ago*, and *The Great Plains*.

Choice of embroidery threads available from your favorite distributor:

Sulky® of America

www.sulky.com

1-800-874-4115

# Family Support:

A very special thanks to my husband, Mark. I appreciate the never-ending support and encouragement you've given me over the years. Another special thanks to my sons, Brad and Chad, and their wives, Jami and Jennifer, and granddaughter, Quinne. You all bring so much joy and happiness to my life.

Thank you to a few of my very special friends— my sisters, Dianne Pauls and Elizabeth Krautbauer—and my mother, Pat Segner, for all of your help, creative input, and outdoor fun.